REVELATION THEOLOGY

REVELATION THEOLOGY

A History

AVERY DULLES

A CROSSROAD BOOK
THE SEABURY PRESS · NEW YORK

The Seabury Press
815 Second Avenue
New York, N.Y. 10017

ISBN: 0-8164-1112-3
Library of Congress Catalog Card Number: 70–81381
© 1969 by Herder and Herder, Inc.
Manufactured in the United States of America

CONTENTS

To my colleagues and students
at Woodstock College
on the occasion
of its centenary year
1969

INTRODUCTION

In undertaking to compose a brief history of Christian views of revelation, the author is conscious of a methodological difficulty. Should one presuppose some definite notion of revelation? If this is done, there is a risk that the whole survey will be prejudiced by a view that is partial and to some extent personal. But if no clear notion is presupposed, it would seem impossible to decide what ought to be included in the survey. In practice we shall discuss that which has popularly gone by the name of revelation or has been regarded as such by significant Christian thinkers. Only after the survey is complete will it be possible to take an informed stand on what the true nature of revelation is.

At the outset it may be well to point out the well known fact that the word "revelation" is derived from the Latin *revelare,* which in turn corresponds to the Greek *apokalyptein.* Both these terms signify, etymologically, to remove a veil (*velum, kalymma*); thus, to unveil or disclose. In common usage, even outside a religious context, revelation usually implies a sudden or unexpected receipt of knowledge of a profoundly significant character—especially that which gives the recipient a new outlook on, and attitude towards, life and the world. It frequently designates the action whereby one person freely confides his intimate thoughts and sentiments to another, thereby enabling the latter to enter into his spiritual world.

In a general way we may say that in Christian religious parlance revelation means a free manifestation by God of that which lies beyond the normal reach of human inquiry. It is the initial action by which God emerges from his hiddenness, calls to man, and invites him to a covenant-existence.

Revelation is of constitutive importance for the whole Christian life. The act of faith, which is man's positive response to revelation, is viewed in most theological traditions as the "foundation and source of all justification" (see Trent, *DS* 1532; Vatican I, *DS* 3008). Faith goes out to God inasmuch as he has revealed himself and things pertinent to man's religious life. Christian conduct is regulated, in great part, by what is believed to be divinely revealed.

Revelation is, moreover, of fundamental significance to theology—for theology has been well defined as "faith seeking understanding." The theologian, however, cannot be content to analyze and present some abstract concept of revelation in isolation from the rest of reality. He must confront revelation in the concrete shape and circumstances in which it comes to man, and reflect on its relationship to the totality of that which he knows, or thinks he knows. It would be insufficient, therefore, to define theology as the science of revelation.

In the following pages an effort will be made to outline, in some kind of historical sequence, what influential Christian theologians of various traditions have understood by revelation. This survey seeks to reflect the attitude enunciated by Paul VI in his opening address at the second session of Vatican II: "We look with reverence upon the true religious patrimony we share in common, which has been preserved and in part even well developed among our separated brethren" (see *AAS* 55 [1963] 853f.).

This history contains lacunae, partly because of the author's desire to be brief, partly because of the limited scope of his knowledge, and partly because it seemed best to concentrate on certain critical turning points, especially those of greatest significance for the current situation of theology in Western Europe and North America. In a longer survey it would surely be desirable to include some discussion of the Orthodox tradition, and perhaps especially of Russian religious thinkers such as Sergius Bulgakov and Nikolai Berdyaev, who have made notable contributions to the theology of revelation in our own century.

The same is obviously true of Jewish theologians such as Martin Buber and Abraham Heschel.

While primarily intended to clarify the notion of revelation, this survey aims also to shed some light on the nature of the theological process. In the course of these pages it should become evident that theologians have never thrived as lonely pioneers; they have progressed through earnest and committed dialogue with their predecessors and contemporaries. Every individual thinker has his limitations and blind spots; only through exposure to many voices and points of view can one hope to neutralize these deficiencies, and gain some intimations of the full scope of revelation. We must therefore let our fellow believers—and even those whose beliefs or unbelief we cannot share—challenge and instruct us. The creative theologian is never content either to ignore others or to repeat verbatim what they have said. He seeks to sift out what seems valid and relevant, and to develop, in the light of his own problems and perspectives, the ideas which he sees struggling to be born in the words of others. In this sense, theology is a maieutic process.

If the reader comes to this sketch with eagerness to formulate a correct definition of revelation, he may gradually become convinced that no one definition could possibly do justice to a reality so rich and many-sided. Every definition is necessarily abstract; it confronts its subject matter with a particular outlook, a particular concern, and a particular conceptual framework. While this is legitimate, it should not cause us to forget that revelation itself, as a concrete and mysterious self-communication of the divine, cannot be circumscribed by any definition. It is apprehended as much through significant facts, intuitions of value, and symbolic imagery as through clear and distinct ideas.

It may be hoped, therefore, that the tale of what various eminent Christians have had to say about revelation may illuminate the mystery in a manner at least as satisfying as any single definition formulated within the limited perspectives of a particular systematic approach.

The author wishes to express his gratitude to Professor John

11

Macquarrie of Union Theological Seminary, New York City,
for having made a number of helpful suggestions on the treatment of Protestant and Anglican theologians in these pages,
and to Mrs. Nancy Blunt for having typed the entire manuscript.

1. BIBLICAL VIEWS
OF REVELATION

A. The Old Testament

No sophisticated reader today needs to be told that the Old Testament did not drop down ready-made from heaven. It recounts the stages by which a people, originally rather primitive and barbaric, were gradually educated in the ways of God. Christians find in it a divinely intended record of the providential process by which Israel was gradually led toward the fullness of revelation in Christ.

Just as we have preparatory revelation in the Old Testament —in some cases very inadequately grasped by a "stiff-necked" people—so too we have preparatory ideas of revelation. The Old Testament contains legends and sagas which would not pass any contemporary tests for historical accuracy. It likewise preserves here and there the traces of primitive mythical thinking. None of it is the work of critically reflective minds in the modern sense. For the Christian, moreover, the Old Testament does not rank as a revelation complete is itself, but only as a part of the whole process of revelation leading up to the New Testament. Conversely, the New Testament does not stand by itself; it is organically linked to the Old Testament as the matrix out of which it grows. The same themes are resumed and amplified on continually higher planes until at length all the lines converge in Christ, who in turn illumines—and is illumined by—the entire prehistory that points toward him, though in a veiled manner.

In the Old Testament, which in some respects resembles a

great museum, we find a fascinating variety of conceptions about revelation. In some of the early books we may detect evidences of superstitious resort to magical practices—divination, dreams, lots, and omens. In facing decisions regarding wars, alliances, and internal political matters, the Israelite leaders were accustomed to consult Yahweh; and this in practice meant obtaining oracular statements from the priests. The priest would normally don a kind of waistcloth called the "ephod" and employ mysterious instruments known as the "urim and thummim"—possibly small sticks or stones which were so marked as to indicate affirmative or negative replies (see Ex. 28:30; 1 Sam. 30:7f., and so forth). Israel differed markedly from other nations in the ancient Near East in that it did not indulge in elaborate divinatory techniques such as hepatoscopy. Still more remarkable is the Israelite prohibition of images, which most of the surrounding nations regarded as principal bearers of revelation.

Especially in the patriarchal period, great attention was given to dreams as vehicles of revelation. Joseph is prominent as an interpreter of dreams. Influenced perhaps by Egyptian practice, he also makes use of a cup for divination (Gen. 44:5). But in all this there is nothing peculiarly Israelitic. In order to grasp the specifically Israelite view of revelation we must turn our attention to the historical events in which, according to the biblical view, the nation received the cardinal ideas that shaped its corporate life. Several stages of this salvation history, as reflected in the biblical tradition, may be singled out as decisive.[1]

1. *The Call of Abraham* (Gen. 12:1–7). The call comes to Abram quite suddenly, it would appear. This revelation, so far as the records disclose, did not rest upon previous events. It is sheer promise, and looks forward to a future fulfilment that is to answer the present word and thus complete the revelation itself by a concrete historical embodiment. The revelation involves Abraham in a partnership with Yahweh, and in this covenant Abraham's posterity is destined to share (see Gen. 17:1–4).

1. In the following division I have been influenced by R. Latourelle, *Theology of Revelation* (Staten Island, 1966) 22–29.

14

In the revelation to Abraham attention is focussed on the word, which comes gratuitously because God in his mercy wishes to call a particular people to a happier destiny. There are "theophanies" in the Abraham cycle, such as the apparition of the three men in Gen. 18:1ff., but in these stories attention is concentrated not on the visible manifestation but on the word. God appears in order to speak, and his word is given to inaugurate a new era of history.

In later patriarchal narratives, such as the stories of Isaac, Jacob, and Joseph, God continues to show his favor to Abraham's posterity and thus proves his fidelity to his pledged word.

2. *Exodus and Sinai.* This is unquestionably the central event in the Old Testament, and hence commends itself to special scrutiny. The cycle begins with the "inaugural vision" and the call of Moses in Exodus 3. The attention of Moses is drawn by a theophany, the symbolic vision of the burning bush. The sign is a miraculous one: the bush, though afire, is not consumed. But God, here again, appears only in order to speak. He identifies himself historically as the God of Abraham, Isaac, and Jacob, and goes far beyond all previous self-revelations by imparting knowledge of his own name (Yahweh). The vision both looks back to patriarchal times and points forward in hope to the future. God's speech is, as in the case of Abraham, a summons to action. Moses is called to play a decisive role in salvation history. The ultimate aim of this revelation, as of others, is soteriological. Most proximately, it aims to liberate Israel from its Egyptian servitude.

The theophany of Mount Sinai completes what was begun in the initial call of Moses. In Exodus 19:ff. Moses receives God's law for his people amid thunder and lightning, clouds of smoke and trumpet blasts. The revelation essentially consists not in these phenomena but in the word of God: the ten *debarim* (words) of the Law. And the purpose of the Law is to bring the whole people into a covenant relationship with Yahweh so that they may indeed be "my very own out of all the peoples . . . , a kingdom of priests, a holy nation" (Ex. 19:5f.). Thus the Sinai

15

revelation is ultimately directed to the entire nation and is intended for their salvation.

3. *The Prophets.* In a wide sense of the term, Moses himself is a prophet, and he might indeed be called the very prototype of Old Testament prophecy, insofar as he has a direct and familiar relationship to God. Whereas other prophets may know God in dreams and visions, Moses is privileged to speak to him face to face (Num. 12:6ff.).

In Old Testament usage, the term *nabi* (a term of obscure etymology which is generally translated "prophet") covers a wide variety of personages who receive divine communications and inform others of God's hidden plans and emotions. In the earlier traditions preserved for us in the books of Samuel and Kings, we learn of "speaking prophets," such as Samuel, Nathan, Elijah, and Elisha. They are gifted with clairvoyance and frequently fall into ecstasies; many of them also perform remarkable miracles. Some of the prophets of this period entered prophetic guilds (the "sons of the prophets") which seem to have been, in part, hereditary.

In the eighth and seventh centuries, with the advent of the so-called "writing prophets," prophecy receives what is often referred to as its "classical" form. Clairvoyance and other preternatural phenomena become rarer, and prophecy assumes more clearly its religious role of recalling the nation to fidelity to its covenant promises. Sixteen of our biblical books—the four major (Isaiah, Jeremiah, Ezekiel, Daniel) and the twelve minor prophets—are attributed to prophetic authorship. The greater part of these books, it would seem, were written not by the prophets themselves, but by their disciples.

As a study of these works will show, prophecy does not essentially consist in the prediction of future events. The prophets are God's spokesmen, who receive his word, and pass it on for weal or woe. They are, par excellence, the mediators of the word, and in view of the central place of the word of God in the Israelite view of revelation, special attention must be given to the prophets for a biblical theology of revelation.

The prophets commonly attribute their calling to a sudden

16

action on the part of God, not preceded by any kind of human preparation. This call revolutionized their lives, and demanded utter obedience on their part. A number of rather detailed descriptions of the prophetic call are preserved in the Old Testament. Isaiah in chapter 6 tells of his inaugural vision, including the cleansing of his lips by a burning coal. Jeremiah, in the opening chapter of his work, attributes his vocation to a sovereignly free choice on the part of God: "Before I formed you in the womb I knew you, and before you were born I consecrated you; I appointed you a prophet to the nations" (Jer. 1:5). When the prophet remonstrates that he is only a youth, the Lord exhorts him to courage: "Behold, I have put my words in your mouth. See, I have set you this day over nations and over kingdoms, to pluck up and to break down, to destroy and to overthrow, to build and to plant" (1:9–10). The prophet's word is powerful since it participates in the omnipotence of God, from whom it comes.

In numerous Old Testament passages allusion is made to severe bodily effects that ensue from the prophetic vision. Ezekiel describes how he sat on the ground overwhelmed for seven days after his call (Ezek. 3:15). Daniel testifies that after one of his visions he was left pale and trembling, and fell into a deep slumber (10:8f.). On another occasion (8:27) he was overcome and lay sick for some days. Isaiah writes that his loins were filled with anguish, and that pangs seized him like those of a woman in childbirth (21:3). Jeremiah gives a poignant description of how the prophet feels the power of the word within him, demanding utterance. "There is in my heart as it were a burning fire shut up in my bones, and I am weary with holding it in, and I cannot" (20:9). While these descriptions are in some cases pseudonymous, and are presumably influenced by stylistic conventions, they undoubtedly contain some valid historical indications of the revelatory experiences of the Hebrew prophets.

Accompanied though it is with unusual psychic phenomena, the prophetic message, at least in the classical prophets, does not have to do with recondite matters pertaining to the world

17

beyond. Unlike many of the medieval mystics, who preferred the cloister, the prophets were normally concerned with political and military matters and participated actively in national affairs. The content of their message reflects a keen perception of the contemporary historical situation, appraised in the light of the Covenant, and does not impart information that would seem to be intrinsically beyond the realm of natural knowledge.[2] When the prophets use promises and threats they do so not in order to show their clairvoyant powers, but in order to bring about repentance and reform.

4. *Deuteronomy.* The Deuteronomic literature of the eighth century, which seems to reflect a confluence of the priestly and prophetic currents in the Northern Kingdom, represents a new stage in the theology of revelation. Deuteronomy extends the concept of the "word of God" to include the whole corpus of Israelite legislation—religious, civil, and criminal—rather than just the original ten "words" of Sinai, or even the messages of the prophets. The *torah,* attributed in its entirety to the great legislator, Moses, is presented not simply as a set of abstract regulations, but as an effective vehicle of God's will, which it makes present to men. "The word is very near you; it is in your mouth and in your heart, so that you can do it" (Deut. 30:14).

The Deuteronomic interpretation of history dominates a number of the historical books (including Judges, Samuel, and Kings), which portray the course of events as the working out in time of the covenant relationship between God and Israel. The idea of history as a medium by which God manifests his attributes and attitudes may be found in some of the most ancient creedal statements embedded in Deuteronomy (for example, 26:5–6). Elsewhere, history is viewed as the effective unfolding of the promises and threats previously contained in God's word. As time goes on, the hopes of Israel gradually become centered on the monarchy, which is made a center of cult. The books of Chronicles, from another point of view than the

2. Such is the view defended by J. Lindblom, *Prophecy in Ancient Israel* (Oxford, 1963) 199.

Deuteronomic writings, seek to legitimate the cultic offices founded by David.

5. *Messianic and Apocalyptic Expectations.* In much of the historical literature the Davidic dynasty is idealized with strong religious overtones. As the fortunes of this dynasty fade under the divided monarchy, the prophets focus the expectations of Israel on some great future intervention of God analogous to his past actions. A blessed era is foretold in which there is to be a new David, a new Moses, a new Covenant, or a new Exodus.

This eschatological Messianism, which reaches its highest expression in Deutero-Isaiah and Jeremiah, to some degree prepares for a new form of revelational literature. Apocalyptic, which becomes widespread under the depressing circumstances of the Babylonian Captivity and the Maccabean period, is exemplified by Daniel and much of the intertestamental literature. Unlike classical prophecy, apocalyptic ceases to look upon the catastrophes of history as effects of God's punitive will; indeed, it abandons all effort to find meaning in history. "History, so far from being the medium in which religious ideas could be expressed, had become literally a marking time until the eschaton should come."[3]

The view of revelation characteristic of the Apocalypses, while differing sharply from the prophetic, in some ways resembles the sapiential. The apocalyptic seers seek to interpret dreams and visions and thus to penetrate the secret counsels of God. Unlike prophecy, which is proclaimed openly to all, apocalyptic makes much of esoteric knowledge.

6. *Wisdom Literature.* Since much of the Israelite sapiential material consists of collections of homely maxims built upon experience and common prudence, this brand of literature might be thought not to pertain to revelation. But the older traditions look upon wisdom as a charism bestowed at God's good pleasure. In the patriarchal stories, Joseph is depicted as outstripping the sages of Israel thanks to the illuminations imparted to him from on high (Gen. 41:16.38). Later, Solomon is held forth as a prod-

3. Stanley B. Frost, "Apocalyptic and History," in J. Philip Hyatt (ed.), *The Bible in Modern Scholarship* (Nashville, 1965) 110.

19

igy of inspired sagacity (1 Kings 4:29). Job's would-be comforter, Eliphaz, attributes his counsel to direct inspiration from heaven. In fact, as Gerhard von Rad observes,[4] he gives the fullest description of the psychology of prophetic revelation that occurs in the Old Testament (Job 4:12–17).

The great wisdom collections, such as Proverbs, Qoheleth, Sirach, and Wisdom, while resting upon ancient sources, were compiled in the Persian and Hellenistic periods. The editors, convinced that all human wisdom comes from God and that the summit of wisdom consists in obedience to him, interpret the patterns of experience in the light of their religious faith. Insofar as this Jewish wisdom rests unequivocally on the self-manifestation of God through history, prophecy, and law, it too may be said to contain revelation, at least indirectly, by reflection.

7. *Psalms.* According to our modern way of thinking, we should be inclined to say that the Psalms should be reckoned not as revelation, but as a human response to it. But this distinction is perhaps artificial since it may be argued that revelation does not achieve itself until it is formulated in human words. In any case, the Israelites saw a close link between prophecy and psalmody, as may be seen, for instance, in the canticles of the prophetesses Miriam (Ex. 15:20–21) and Deborah (Judg. 5). In the last words of David, as narrated in 2 Samuel, the "sweet psalmist of Israel" claims inspiration for himself: "The Spirit of the Lord speaks by me, his word is upon my tongue" (23:2). As inspired hymns of prayer and praise, the psalms are revelatory to us—as they were to the Israelites—of the power, majesty, and fidelity of God, which they celebrate. Many of the psalms incorporate oracles and responses from Yahweh into their structure.

Summarizing the Old Testament view of revelation, one may say that Yahweh progressively manifests himself, through word and work, as Lord of history. He freely raises up spokesmen of his own choosing, whether patriarchs such as Abraham, na-

---

4. G. von Rad, *Old Testament Theology* 1 (New York, 1962) 101; also 2 (New York, 1965) 68.

tional heroes such as Moses, or prophets and seers such as Samuel, Isaiah, and Ezekiel. He entrusts them with messages which they are to deliver to others, often to the whole people. Although the universal significance of Israelite religion is sometimes suggested (especially in Deutero-Isaiah), the horizons are for the most part particular, insofar as the revelation is addressed to a single nation. The Israelite faith is also inchoative, insofar as it is in tension toward a greater and definitive manifestation yet to come. While often accompanied by miraculous theophanies, dreams, and visions, revelation for the Old Testament writers is primarily to be found in the "word of God." The word, however, is not mere speculative speech. It refers to the concrete history of Israel, which it recalls and interprets. It commemorates God's previous dealings with his people and includes promises for the future, thus arousing faith and hope. The word of God, moreover, is powerful and dynamic; it produces a transforming encounter with the Lord who utters it, and imposes stringent demands on the recipient. It opens up to him a new way of life, pregnant with new possibilities of punishment and deliverance. Revelation is ultimately aimed to bring blessings upon the whole nation, including peace, prosperity, and holiness.

B. The New Testament

As in other matters, so in the notion of revelation, the New Testament takes up the themes enunciated in the Old Testament, draws them together, and brings them to a higher and unforseen fulfilment. "All these writings of ancient Israel, both those which are concerned with her past relationship to God and those which dealt with her future one, were seen by Jesus Christ, and certainly by the Apostles and the early Church, as a collection of predictions which pointed to him, the saviour of Israel and of the world."[5] The heart of the New Testament is that the definitive, universal revelation is given to mankind in Jesus, to

5. Ibid., 2, 319.

be authoritatively proclaimed by the Church to all nations until the end of time (Mt. 28:18–20). The Old Testament affirmation that God spoke to man "face to face, as a man speaks to his friend" (Ex. 33:11) was surpassingly fulfilled in the coming of God's own Son (Jn. 1:17–18). The best summary of the New Testament view of revelation, as related to the Old Testament, is Hebrews 1:1–2: "In many and various ways God spoke of old to our fathers by the prophets; but in these last days he has spoken to us by a Son, whom he appointed the heir of all things, through whom also he created the world."

In the *Synoptic Gospels,* which concentrate on the ministry of Jesus, revelation is chiefly understood as something which Jesus communicates through his preaching and teaching. As a preacher, Jesus, like John the Baptist, heralds the imminent arrival of the Kingdom of God. He points to his cures and exorcisms as evidences that Satan's dominion is being overthrown and that God's rulership is being established. In his capacity as teacher, Jesus gives more detailed and continuous instruction, especially to his chosen disciples. By faith in Jesus, the disciples are initiated into the mystery that will be fully disclosed when the Son of Man appears in glory.

Is Jesus regarded as a prophet? He is occasionally hailed by this title, and even (with an implied reference to the prediction of the "new Moses" in Deut. 18:18) as *the* prophet. But the evangelists and apostles do not ascribe this title to Jesus, nor does he himself seem to have been satisfied with it. The designation fails to do justice to the transcendence of his person and of his mission—aspects far better expressed by the term "Son." In his role as Son he has intimate knowledge of the Father that enables him to be the revealer par excellence: "No one knows the Son except the Father, and no one knows the Father except the Son and anyone to whom the Son chooses to reveal him" (Mt. 11:27).

Jesus as Son is thus the revealer of the Father and his plans. The central theme of the revelation is the arrival of the Kingdom, which is understood as involving all the blessings foretold by the Law, the Prophets, and the Psalms. The apostles are the chosen recipients of this revelation, notwithstanding their lack of personal qualifications (Mt. 11:25). They are freely called by Jesus, enlightened by the grace of the Father (Mt. 16:17), instructed by Jesus regarding the true nature of the Kingdom, and appointed to go and preach in his name.

Within this general framework, common to all the Synoptics, each evangelist presents the revelation of Jesus with a particular nuance of his own.

Mark has been aptly dubbed by Dibelius and Bultmann the "book of secret epiphanies." For Mark the words and deeds of Jesus have a paradoxical quality. They reveal and yet they conceal. They manifest the messiahship of Jesus in a way that produces, for the most part, only bewilderment and disorientation. The disciples are stupid and obtuse; the parables are confusing; the miracles are uncanny; the more striking of them are to be kept secret until the Son of Man has risen from the dead. At the climax of the gospel, a Roman centurion who has seen and heard nothing wonderful from Jesus himself except his dying cry proclaims with a sudden burst of faith that Jesus is indeed the Son of God. Later an angel announces that Jesus has arisen from the tomb. But the women to whom the angel brings these tidings say nothing, for they are afraid. And at this point the gospel abruptly ends (for Mk. 16:9–16 is a later addition, apparently by another hand). In this disconcerting gospel the revelation brought by Jesus is presented as awesome, haunting, or, to use Rudolf Otto's term, "numinous."[6]

Matthew puts the accent not on kerygma but on catechesis. Jesus is depicted as the new Moses who promulgates from the Mount the new and perfect law of charity. In the long sermons and moral instructions characteristic of this gospel, revelation appears as a code of behavior for those who enter the Kingdom. Written about the time that the rabbis were engaged in codifying the traditions of Judaism at Jamnia, Matthew may be said to offer a kind of anti-rabbinical rabbinism, in which the precepts of the Mosaic law are heightened, universalized, and

6. Cf. T. A. Burkill, *Mysterious Revelation: An Examination of the Philosophy of St. Mark's Gospel* (Ithaca, 1963).

23

interiorized. In the face of modern existential interpretations of revelation, the Matthean gospel affords striking evidence that "For some in the primitive Church, if not for all, the penetrating demands of Jesus, no less than the great kerygmatic affirmations about him, were part of the 'bright light of the Gospel,' that is, they were revelatory."[7]

Luke, as the theologian of history, is concerned with the change of aeons that occurred in Christ. The old era, which leads up to the Baptist, is at an end. Jesus comes, and prays, and the Spirit descends upon him. Driven by the Spirit, he powerfully proclaims that the messianic promises of Isaiah have come to fulfilment in his own person. More than any other New Testament author, Luke hangs his conception of revelation on a theology of history, with special emphasis on the Holy Spirit as the gift of God in Christ.[8]

Acts is a further development of the Lukan theology of history. Taking for granted that the basic revelation has already been given in Jesus' public and risen life, it shows how the apostles as chosen witnesses (especially Peter and Paul) spread the good news from Jerusalem outward through Judea and Samaria, and far into the Greco-Roman world. This entire operation unfolds under the impetus of the Holy Spirit, who intervenes continually in the life of the infant Church. The visions and ecstasies of the apostles (such as those of Paul and Peter in Acts 9 and 10) may be viewed as a further outpouring of the Pentecostal Spirit, supplementing the previous revelations in the words and deeds of Jesus.

Paul offers a rich and complex doctrine of revelation, which it would take many pages to expound. On the one hand he looks on revelation as something charismatically received through the miraculous action of the Holy Spirit within the apostolic community even after the departure of the risen Lord (dreams and visions, locutions, and glossalalia). On the other hand he

7. W. D. Davies, *The Setting of the Sermon on the Mount* (Cambridge, Eng., 1964) 437.

8. Cf. Hans Conzelmann, *The Theology of St. Luke* (New York, 1961).

repeatedly insists that the preaching and faith of the Church must be regulated by the gospel, of which he and the other apostles are judges. While he looks on himself as an apostle by reason of the direct revelation he received at Damascus and the mandate he received from the risen Lord to preach to the gentiles, he acknowledges the authority of Peter and the other "pillars" at Jerusalem, and is anxious to maintain solidarity with them (Gal. 2:1–10).

The content of revelation for Paul is, most briefly, the *mystērion*—that is, the redemptive counsel of God which has hitherto been kept secret. Now at last God has promulgated his astonishing plan—obscurely foretold by the prophets—to offer salvation to all mankind, independently of observance of the Law, through faith in the crucified and risen Jesus. This revelation is something to be proclaimed to all the nations as the glad tidings of salvation. It is God's word, a word to be accepted in faith and obedience. Far from being a mere body of doctrine, it is "the power of God for salvation to everyone who has faith, to the Jew first and also to the Greek" (Rom. 1:16).

Although the notion of apostolic tradition (*paradosis*) already occurs in the earlier Pauline epistles (2 Thess. 2:15; 1 Cor. 11), the Pastorals particularly stress the concept of revelation as a deposit (*parathēkē*) to be faithfully safeguarded and handed on (1 Tim. 6:20; 2 Tim. 1:12.14). We shall see this notion of the *depositum fidei* later taken up in the documents of the Church.

John, although he never uses the term *apokalyptein* except in an Old Testament citation, develops a powerful theology of revelation in terms of his doctrine concerning the Logos, testimony, and enlightenment.[9] In his prologue he identifies Christ the Son of God with the divine Logos, thus giving a new meaning to the term "word of God," which elsewhere in the New Testament is generally a synonym for the "gospel."

More strongly than other New Testament authors, John accents the idea of testimony, developing the notion in a juridical

9. Cf. W. K. M. Grossouw, *Revelation and Redemption: A Sketch of the Theology of St. John* (Westminster, Md., 1955).

sense reminiscent of the law courts. Jesus speaks solemnly of what he knows from direct experience, thanks to his intimate life in the "bosom" of the Father. The Son by his words bears witness to the Father, but the Father by his miraculous deeds bears witness to the Son. The Spirit, when he comes, is to bear witness to the Son, and the disciples too are witnesses, for they have been with Jesus from the beginning (15:26–27). Thus the whole process of revelation is a chain of testimony.

The words of Jesus and his mighty works engender faith (14:10–12), but for anyone to believe he must first be drawn by the Father (6:44). To see Jesus is to see the Father (14:9), for the Father and he are one (10:30). The disciples, having seen, heard, and actually touched the "word of life," are charged with proclaiming his word to others, so that they may have fellowship with the Father and the Son (1 Jn. 1:1–3). Revelation, therefore, does not really differ from the gift of eternal life through the Son.

Another theme of great importance in the Johannine theology of revelation is that of light. Christ is the light that shines on all men, but the majority do not come to him. Many in their wickedness prefer to lurk in the darkness. Those who follow Christ are assured of light and life (Jn. 8:12; 12:46). The Spirit of truth abides with the disciples in order to recall to their minds what Jesus has taught, and to guide them into the fullness of truth by saying what the disciples in Jesus' lifetime were not prepared to hear (14:26; 16:12ff.).

The Johannine *Apocalypse* is by definition a revelation (1:1), and stands in the apocalyptic tradition of the late Old Testament and of intertestamental times. Using the literary form of a series of visions, the author shows how the victory of Christ assures the faithful believers that they will emerge victorious from persecution, and will enjoy the fullness of revelation in the heavenly Jerusalem, where the Lamb himself will be the radiant source of light (21:23). The book describes Christ as the "Word of God" (19:13), the "King of kings and Lord of lords" (19:16), and "the Alpha and the Omega"

26

(22:13). Reaching its climax in a description of the final coming of Christ, the book concludes with the aspiration, "Come, Lord Jesus" (22:20).

Finally, the Epistle to the *Hebrews* furnishes us with yet another inspired theology of revelation. Here the prevailing theme is the unity and difference between the two Testaments, each being a revelation of the God who speaks through his word. The word of God, which reaches its completion in Christ as Son, is living, active, sharper than a two-edged sword, so subtle that it penetrates the fine line between soul and spirit, and is able to discern the most hidden thoughts (4:12–13). On the lips of the preacher, the word of God demands ready and instant obedience. "Therefore, as the Holy Spirit says, 'Today, when you hear his voice, do not harden your hearts as in the rebellion' " (3:7f.).

Drawing together the various strands of the New Testament conception of revelation, we may offer the following general description:

(a) It is a completely gratuitous disclosure of God's mind and purposes, salvific in intent. God freely decides to publish the good news of his redemptive will toward all mankind, and raises up "vessels of election" (see Acts 9:15) to herald the message.

(b) The apostles take the place of the prophets as God's chief heralds (Mt. 28:19; Lk. 24:48; Acts 1:8; Jn. 17:20; and so forth).[10]

(c) The revelation is to be proclaimed to all mankind, as is evident from the same texts. To the universality of the gospel there corresponds a universal need on the part of mankind. Although in times past God may have been satisfied with a vague and undetermined kind of worship, which attained God only as one unknown (Acts 17:23.30–31), now the time has come for

10. Concerning the complicated question who ranked as an apostle, see Béda Rigaux, O.F.M., "The Twelve Apostles," in H. Küng (ed.), *Apostolic Succession: Rethinking a Barrier to Unity* (*Concilium* 34) (Glen Rock, N.J., 1968) 5–15.

men to repent and to call upon Jesus as universal Saviour (Rom. 10:12–18; Rom. 16:26; 1 Tim. 2:3–7).[11]

(d) The revelation is final, in the sense that it fulfils the whole economy of the Old Testament and ushers in the last age of the world (Heb. 1:1–2; Eph. 1:10). Believing Christians have already received this revelation (Rom. 16:25f.; 1 Cor. 2:10; Eph. 3:3.5). Yet revelation continues to occur, insofar as we are still living in the last times (1 Cor. 14:30; Phil. 4:15; Jn. 16:13). So obscure is our apprehension of the divine truth in this life, that it falls far short of the face-to-face vision for which we hope (1 Cor. 13:12). In many New Testament texts, therefore, the term "reveal" is used in the future tense, with reference to the consummation of history, including the revelation of the man of sin (2 Thess. 2:3.8) and the return of the Son of Man (Lk. 17:30). In the "Day of the Lord," as understood by Paul, there will be a revelation of God's wrath against sinners (Rom. 2:5), the salvation of the faithful (Rom. 8:19), and the glory of Christ with his saints (Col. 3:4; 2 Thess. 1:10). In Johannine language, the life which is announced by the witnesses of Christ will not be seen as it truly is until he appears at the end (1 Jn. 3:2).

(e) The revelation is communicated through a combination of words and deeds. Paul and Hebrews accentuate the idea that revelation is a word demanding the obedience of faith. Yet, in the gospels, Christ reveals not only by his preaching and teaching (Mk. 1:14f.; Jn. 6:63.14:10), but also by his symbolic actions, such as cleansing the Temple, embracing little children, cursing the barren fig tree, and the like. Many of his miracles, such as the multiplication of the loaves and fishes, and the healing of the deaf mute, may be regarded as parables in action. From the point of view of faith, all that Christ did is instructive and revelatory. As Augustine put it in a famous text, "Because Christ himself is the Word of God, the very deed of the Word is a word to us."[12]

11. On this point see further Bertil Gärtner, *The Areopagus Speech and Natural Revelation* (Uppsala, 1955).
12. *Tract. in Ioh.* 24:1 (*CC* 36:244).

28

More than this, we may say that in Christ the relation of word and work becomes close to the point of identity. In his character as Logos he is the subsistent Word, the intelligible reflection of the invisible God. In his flesh he is the sacrament of God—the *verbum visibile Patris,* as Irenaeus would later put it.

It is often said that Jesus Christ, as the Incarnate Word, is subsistent revelation. This statement has good scriptural support (see 2 Cor. 4:4–6; Heb. 1:1–2), but it must be properly understood. He is not revelation for us except insofar as his inner secret becomes manifest through his words and deeds, and through the communication of his Spirit to those who believe. The revelation which he bears actually becomes revelation insofar as he is recognized as Son and Redeemer. In his earthly life, Jesus was supremely docile to the entire tradition of Israel and to the inspirations of the Holy Spirit. In his risen life he appears as one who is no longer picking his way, but has arrived at a full and pacific enjoyment of God's presence.

While the New Testament is mainly interested in Jesus as active agent in revelation, it seems biblically correct to look upon him also as the supreme recipient of revelation. The Apocalypse (1:1) speaks of "the revelation of Jesus Christ which God gave *him.*" In the baptismal scene at the Jordan, the Synoptics portray Jesus as seeing the heavens opened and the Spirit descending upon him in the form of a dove. The message, "Thou art my beloved Son, in thee I am well pleased" (Mk. 1:11; Lk. 3:22; but see Mt. 3:17 for a different version!) comes to Jesus himself. Mark does not even fear to report limitations on Jesus' revealed knowledge (Mk. 13:32). Luke seems at one point to attribute to Jesus a mysterious vision of Satan's fall (Lk. 10:18 as interpreted by J. M. Creed and others). In the Fourth Gospel, Jesus proclaims, "I preach only what the Father has taught me" (Jn. 8:28), a statement which seems to imply that Jesus first receives the message which he is to transmit to others. But there are other passages in the New Testament which have been interpreted as denying that Jesus receives revelation.

To reconcile the various texts in the light of a more developed doctrinal teaching is an important task for Christology.

The role of Jesus is not unimportant for the general theory of revelation. Too often the theory of revelation has taken its start from the transmission of revelation by the Church, without sufficient attention to the question how revelation was originally received. Some authors naïvely say that it was simply "given" to the Church by inspired prophets and the Son of God, without attending to the complex question of how it came into the human mind of these mediators. Once the focus of interest is shifted to the original acquisition of revelation, it becomes possible to relate revealed knowledge more meaningfully to the total religious quest of mankind.

We have surveyed the Old and New Testaments primarily for positive indications of what the Christian can accept as revelation. But it would be possible also to survey the same sources for indications of what revelation is not. Errors regarding revelation are as old as revelation itself. The prophets of Israel had to contend with superstitious divinatory practices and to silence false prophets who pretended to speak in God's name without having been sent. In the New Testament, Paul had to condemn charismatic excesses, which led to disorder and disedification in community worship (1 Cor. 14). The Pastoral Epistles warn against teachers who would substitute vain and curious speculations for the sobriety of the Christian gospel. The Johannine writings warn the faithful not to be taken in by pseudo-prophets who deny that Jesus Christ has come in the flesh (1 Jn. 4:1–2). These heresies, already condemned in the New Testament, have led some scholars to speak of a first-century Christian Gnosticism. Whether or not this term can be justified, it is certain, as we shall see, that Gnosticism became a major heresy in the second century, and thus contributed to the Church's articulation of its own doctrine concerning revelation.

30

2. CHRISTIANITY: THE FIRST EIGHTEEN CENTURIES

Since revelation did not emerge as a major theological theme until after the Enlightenment, it may suffice to give a very cursory survey of the first eighteen centuries. In most of the early theologians, as in the Bible itself, there is no systematic doctrine of revelation. Although the word appears here and there, it is rarely used with the technical meaning it has acquired in modern theology. In order to give a satisfactory account of the theology of revelation implicit in the teaching of the Fathers and Doctors of the Church, one would have to analyze their entire system, which would obviously be beyond our present scope. We shall therefore limit our attention to certain key points that are especially significant for the subsequent history of theology in the nineteenth and twentieth centuries.

A. The Patristic Period

The doctrine of revelation in the Church Fathers and early ecclesiastical writers appears for the most part indirectly in their polemical works. Against the Jews they sought to establish that Jesus had fulfilled the Old Testament prophecies, and was therefore the expected Messiah. Against the pagans they tried to prove that he fulfilled and surpassed the wisdom and piety contained in pagan philosophy and religion. While engaged with these non-Christian adversaries, the Fathers were simultaneously occupied with the refutation of various heresies that

31

sprang up within the Christian fold, the most important of which was Gnosticism.

Christian Gnosticism came into its own in the second century, under such masters as Basilides and Valentinus. Gnosticism was fundamentally an attack on the orthodox view of revelation. In the opinion of one eminent scholar: "The Gnostics endeavored to create a Christianity which, fitting into the culture of the time, would absorb the religious myths of the Orient and give the dominant role to the religious philosophy of the Greeks, to leave but a small place for revelation as the foundation of all theological knowledge, for faith, and for the Gospel of Jesus Christ."[1] While this may be true enough from the standpoint of orthodox Catholicism, it is only fair to note that the Gnostics were deeply concerned with revelation as they understood it. Many of them looked upon Jesus as a teacher sent from heaven to deliver a body of saving doctrines (*gnosis*) for the salvation of those who had within them a spark of the divine spiritual substance, and were thus capable of being reintegrated with the godhead. This saving doctrine, according to some Gnostics, was handed down not so much in written Scriptures as in esoteric tradition.

The second-century heretic Marcion, who had close affinities with Gnosticism, maintained, on the basis of a dualistic cosmology, that the creator-god of the Old Testament was a mere demiurge, and that Christ's body was not real but merely apparent (the cardinal tenet of "docetism," as it is called). The Marcionites therefore repudiated the entire Old Testament revelation. They were highly selective in what they chose to accept among those works which the Church at that period was coming to recognize as the New Testament.

Manichaeanism in the third century, originally a pagan sect, contained numerous borrowings from ancient Persian and Chaldean religion. But it claimed to rest primarily upon original revelations vouchsafed to its founder Mani (or Manes) (d. c. 276) in Babylonia. The Christian Manichaeans, like the Gnostics, looked upon the material world as a prison of darkness and

1. Johannes Quasten, *Patrology* 1 (Westminster, Md., 1950) 254.

sought by various practices to escape into the spiritual realm of light.

The Montanist schism, less widespread and influential than Gnosticism or Manichaeanism, emanated from Phrygia in the second century. Montanus and his disciples, including the prophetesses Prisca and Maximilla, spoke in frenzied ecstasies, and set their own utterances on a level above the teaching of the bishops. The fullness of the Spirit, they claimed, had not been communicated through Christ and the apostles, but only through Montanus and his companions, in whom the final age of the Holy Spirit was beginning to dawn.

In response to Judaism, paganism, and heresies such as those just mentioned, the orthodox Fathers began to develop the Catholic doctrine of revelation on the basis of Scripture and Church tradition. Certain high points of their work may appropriately be signalized here.

Justin Martyr, writing in Rome between 150 and 165, set forth the Christian case against Judaism in his *Dialogue with Trypho the Jew,* and in his two *Apologies* attempted to demonstrate the reasonableness of Christianity to the pagans. In the *Apologies* he maintains that the wisdom of the philosophers, such as it was, came through the eternal Logos who was to become man in Jesus Christ. Anticipating what some twentieth-century authors have to say about "anonymous Christianity," Justin makes the startling statement that all who live by reason are in some sense Christians (1 *Apol.* 46), but that those who are ignorant of the incarnate Word, have only a partial knowledge, and therefore fall into many contradictions (2 *Apol.* 8.10).

Later in the second century, Irenaeus of Lyons sought to defend, against various Gnostic sects, the harmony between the Old and New Testaments. In his *Adversus Haereses* he sketches the outlines of a dynamic theology of history which vies with the best in modern biblical theology. God, in his view, gradually educates the human race through the eternal Logos, and prepares men by stages to receive the "solid food" of Christian revelation. Irenaeus recognizes three distinct Testaments prior to Christ: those of Adam, Noah, and Moses. In the fourth

33

Testament, as he calls it, the divine Word himself becomes visible, appearing in the flesh and bringing to a head in his own person the religious history of mankind (the celebrated Irenaean thesis of the recapitulation, or *anakephalaiōsis*). After the Ascension, Christ's visibility is perpetuated in the Church which, though dispersed over the whole earth, believes with one heart and one soul the revelation handed down from the apostles.[2]

Clement of Alexandria (c. 150–c. 213) combines Justin's concern for the values in pagan philosophy with Irenaeus' interest in preserving the Christian meaning of the Old Testament. Clement recognizes three Testaments: pagan philosophy, the Jewish Law, and the Christian Gospel. All three, he argues, derive from one and the same Logos. Just as the Law prepared the Hebrews to accept the teaching of Christ, so philosophy educated the Greeks, predisposing them better to receive the good news of the Gospel. Not only among the Hebrews, but among the Greeks likewise, God stirred up prophets. Christians have the advantage over both Greeks and Jews that they acknowledge as their teacher the Incarnate Logos himself, who illuminates the believing soul with his own incomparable Light. Those who in modern times have been seeking to discover authentic Christian values in the great world religions could greatly profit from a familiarity with what Clement has to say about the mystery religions and philosophies of the Hellenistic world.

The Alexandrian school had its greatest theological genius in the person of Clement's successor, Origen (c. 185–253), justly renowned as a biblical exegete, controversialist, speculative theologian, and spiritual doctor. Like Clement, Origen centers his doctrine of revelation on the divine Logos, whom he regards as the only possible revealer of the Father. In the Old Testament the truth concerning Christ was communicated in a hidden way. Christ at his coming removed the veil. But still the revelation is not manifest to flesh and blood; the gospel must be read in the Spirit. By spiritual purification we approach the full and perfect knowledge which will be given as the "eternal

2. On Irenaeus' doctrine of revelation see the monograph of Juan Ochagavia, *Visible Patris Filius* (Rome, 1964).

gospel" when Christ returns in glory. Origen's profound reflections on the dialectic of Law and Gospel, history and Spirit have continued to inspire many medieval and modern Christians in their efforts to find in the Scriptures a living channel of revelation.

The Alexandrian tradition, auspiciously established by Clement and Origen, was ably continued in the fourth and fifth centuries by Athanasius and Cyril of Alexandria, both of whom wrote eloquently of Christ as the Light of the world[3] and as giver of the Spirit of truth. These authors, of course, are chiefly important for their high Christology, by which they assisted the Church in its struggles, respectively, against Arianism and Nestorianism.

In the latter half of the fourth century a new stimulus to the theology of revelation was provided by the heretical teaching of Eunomius (d. 394), the radical Neo-Arian, who espoused an extreme intellectualism. Maintaining that the supreme Substance consisted in being "unoriginate" (as Newman was to translate the technical term, *aggenētos*), he inferred that God could be perfectly known by the human mind, and thus was not mysterious to those who adhered to the correct doctrine. In reply to Eunomius, the Cappadocian Fathers, especially Basil the Great and his brother Gregory of Nyssa, dwelt on the divine incomprehensibility in a way that contributed permanently to the Christian theology of mystery. Gregory of Nyssa, often called the "founder of mystical theology," maintained that it was possible for a man, after suitable ascetical purification, to discern within himself the image of God's inaccessible beauty.

The Antiochene, St. John Chrysostom (d. 407), contributed to the theology of revelation by his famous homilies *On the Incomprehensibility of God,* which are remarkable for their vivid descriptions of man's sense of holy terror at the approach of the divine. Expatiating on various biblical texts, especially from the book of Daniel, Chrysostom in some ways anticipates the religious phenomenology of Rudolf Otto, and speaks of "fear and

3. On Athanasius see Jaroslav Pelikan, *The Light of the World* (New York, 1962).

trembling" in a way that reminds some readers of Kierkegaard.[4] Also in these sermons, Chrysostom speaks of God's "condescension" (*synkatabasis*) in accommodating his self-manifestation to the weakness of his creatures. Recently Vatican Council II, in its Constitution on Divine Revelation (art. 13), made use of Chrysostom's notion of the divine condescension in order to indicate how the living reality of revelation could be mediated through the human words of those who composed the Bible.

The theology of the Latin West, in its treatment of revelation, was on the whole less speculative than that of the East, and more concerned with the social and juridical aspects of the Church. Some of its initiators, such as Tertullian and Cyprian, gave it a forensic and rhetorical stamp. (Tertullian is famous for his vituperations against Greek philosophy and for his eventual lapse into Montanism.) In the fourth century, Hilary of Poitiers and Ambrose, influenced by the Eastern Fathers, introduced a more contemplative and mystical strain, thus preparing the way for Augustine (354–430), in whom the Western Patristic tradition reaches its highest peak. He combined a vigorous speculative intellect with a deep introspective piety.

For Augustine as for the earlier Church Fathers, Christ is the master of the Old Testament as well as of the New. Augustine distinguishes three main stages in the history of revelation. From Adam until Moses both the Old and the New Testaments were hidden. In the time of Moses, the Old Covenant was made manifest, and in it was hidden the New. Finally, when Christ came, the New Covenant was openly revealed.[5]

In regard to the term "revelation," Augustine uses it at times for extraordinary manifestations such as the visions and ecstasies of which one reads in Holy Scripture. These revelations, he says, could be merely sensory (and thus imperfect) or intellectual (in

4. Regarding these comparisons see Rudolf Otto, *The Idea of the Holy* (New York, paperback, 1958), appendix I, and J. Daniélou's introduction to J. Chrysostom, *Sur l'Incompréhensibilité de Dieu* (*Sources Chrétiennes* 28) (Paris, 1951) 33–45.

5. *De baptismo Libri VII*, 1:24 (*CSEL* 51:168).

which case they were perfect).[6] Augustine also uses the term "revelation" more widely to designate any divine illumination which comes to the mind through prayerful study and consideration of things obscurely known.[7]

Augustine's theology of revelation is closely bound up with his doctrine of illumination, which centers about God as the light of truth. It is not surprising, therefore, that he uses the term "revelation" not so much for the external communication of the gospel as for the inner light by which men are enabled to believe it. In a famous text, Augustine says that the preacher would herald the gospel in vain unless God were to open the hearts of the hearers. "Unless he who dwells within reveals, to what purpose do I speak?"[8]

The following is an excellent summary of Augustine's complex teaching about revelation:

St. Augustine does not treat the idea of revelation *ex professo* any more than the other fathers. The idea, however, is present throughout his work. In Johannine terminology, St. Augustine claims that the vision of God is impossible here below. The Mediator of all revelation is Jesus Christ, Word of God, Son of God, come to manifest through His Words and through His actions, the Gospel of salvation. Still, His message does not achieve its full effect unless man, drawn by the Father, opens his heart to the Word he hears externally. The external Word of Christ and the inspiration of the Spirit compose the one single Word of God. In respect to His role as Revealer, Christ is called Prophet, Lord of the prophets, and primarily Master. He teaches the truth and at the same time He *is* Truth, God revealing and God revealed, God and Way. His doctrine bears upon Himself, for He is in Person the doctrine of the Father, mysteriously revealed. What He reveals is Himself and, through Himself, the love of the Father. The prophets and the apostles share in His light: the light they announce or the light they bear witness to because they have seen and heard. The Word of Christ, object of

6. *Contra Adimantum* 28:2 (*PL* 42:171).
7. *De praedest. sanctorum* 1:1:2 (*PL* 44:962) and 1:4:8 (*PL* 44:916). Other texts to the same effect are cited by Petavius in his *De Incarnatione*, bk. 14, ch. 2, n. 11.
8. *Tract. in Ioh.* 26:7 (*CC* 36:263).

our faith, we can arrive at through the apostolic word, set down in Scripture and proclaimed by the Church. Here below, we walk in faith, but our faith looks to a vision, when the light of the Word will absorb the lesser lights of faith.[9]

The teaching of Augustine dominates the remainder of the Patristic era in the West. After his death his successors, Prosper of Aquitaine (d. c. 463) and Caesarius of Arles (d. 543), relentlessly insisting on the illumination of the Holy Spirit as an indispensable precondition of the act of faith, effectively overcame the Semi-Pelagian heresy. In the latter half of the sixth century, Gregory the Great developed Augustine's doctrine of revelation in a more pastoral direction, especially with regard to the theology of preaching and of prayer.

B. The Middle Ages

The term "revelation," in most of the medieval writers, continues to be used, as in St. Augustine, to designate any kind of divine illumination, including what we should now regard as falling within the ambit of purely natural knowledge. As Congar puts it: "We live [then] in a world in which all the effects that result in true knowledge, and particularly those that rise above ordinary mundane matters, are attributed to God and seen as coming from on high. But they would just as readily be attributed to reason, or to that interior illumination bestowed on us by the Word."[10] Only in the high Scholasticism of the thirteenth century does "revelation" become restricted to strictly supernatural knowledge. In St. Thomas himself, as Congar also notes (p. 124), one may trace a gradual development showing an increasing tendency to restrict *revelatio* to knowledge of a supernatural character and to employ the term in a more objective sense, corresponding to the content of official Church teaching.

9. R. Latourelle, *Theology of Revelation,* 143–44.
10. Y. Congar, *Tradition and Traditions* (New York, 1967) 122. He relies on important articles by de Guibert and de Ghellinck.

Most of the medieval theologians, therefore, have no difficulty in admitting that "revelation," far from having ceased with the apostles, is an ongoing reality in the life of the Church. They are confident that the Holy Spirit is constantly at work in the minds of the faithful, disclosing the intentions of God in their personal lives, and in the Church at large, directing it to a better understanding of its faith and mission. Claude Lejay, at the Council of Trent, echoes the predominant conviction of the preceding millennium when he declares: "In the general councils, the Holy Spirit has revealed to the Church, according to the needs of the time, numerous truths which were not explicitly contained in the canonical books [of Scripture]."[11]

If one were to look for a doctrine of revelation, as the term is currently understood, in the medieval authors, one might be well advised to begin with their statements regarding the relations between faith and reason. For by the object of faith they generally meant approximately that which, in post-Tridentine theology, is called "revelation."

In spite of the fact that nearly every major theologian took a definite position on this disputed point, it is hard to find very satisfying explanations of what they meant by revelation. The reason for this deficiency is no doubt a historical one. The medieval theologians took it for granted that the distinction between faith and reason was clear. Faith, in the objective sense, was identified in their minds with the body of Christian doctrine preached by the Church on the basis of the Bible. And by "reason" they understood, by and large, the heritage of classical pagan culture. Faith was frequently held to be indemonstrable, accepted on authority. Reason was a body of demonstrable truths, attainable by "science" in the Aristotelian sense.

Most of the medieval theologians followed Augustine in his conviction that faith precedes and guides the right use of reason. Such is the view of Johannes Scotus Erigena (c. 810–c. 877), who, however, emphasizes that only under the guidance of faith

11. Görres Gesellschaft (ed.), *Concilium Tridentinum, Tractatuum Pars Prior* 12 (Freiburg im Br., 1930) 523.

does reason fully come into its own. Anselm of Canterbury (1033–1109), though his mentality differed greatly from that of the adventurous Erigena, likewise held for the priority of faith, as is evident from his famous formula, "*Credo ut intelligam.*" Yet Anselm in his way was not exempt from a certain Christian rationalism, for he thought it possible for reason, illuminated by faith, to find demonstrative reasons for the revealed mysteries.

Peter Abelard (c. 1079–1142), who became something of an apostle of Aristotelian logic in his own time, gave a certain priority to reason. Following Justin, he firmly maintained that the pagan philosophers had been divinely enlightened, and were on the true path of salvation. In his *Dialogue Between a Philosopher, a Jew and a Christian,* Abelard addressed himself to the problem of truth in the non-Christian religions, and adopted the position that the Christian faith, understood in a sufficiently comprehensive manner, does not exclude but rather includes the truths to which the pagan and the Jew lay claim. As Gilson has said, "Christian revelation was never, for him, an impassable barrier dividing the chosen from the condemned and truth from error. Abélard knew secret passages from one side to the other and he liked to believe that the Ancients he loved had already found them."[12]

What became for many centuries the standard Catholic view on the relations between faith and reason emerges with greatest clarity in the writings of St. Thomas Aquinas (1225–74). As modes of knowledge, faith and reason are for him diametrically opposed. Reason is an ascending movement of the mind from creatures to God; revelation is a descending action by which the divine truth enters the human mind by a free communication. Revelation, in turn, has two stages. At the first stage, man in this life accepts the divine truth on God's word in faith; then, in the life to come, revelation occurs in the perfect form of vision.[13]

12. Etienne Gilson, *History of Christian Philosophy in the Middle Ages* (New York, 1954) 163.
13. *Summa Contra Gentiles,* bk. 4, ch. 1.

In the very first article of the *Summa Theologica,* Part I, Thomas defines theology as "teaching according to divine revelation" and defends the necessity of theology on the ground that, without divinely communicated knowledge concerning God, as man's last end, man could not properly order his life. Thomas's favorite model for revelation, as it comes to man in this life, is the master-pupil relationship, as appears from the following text:

Man's ultimate beatitude consists in a kind of supernatural vision of God. But man cannot attain to this vision unless he first learns from God as a teacher, as we read in John 6 [v. 45], "Everyone who has listened to the Father, and has learned, comes to me." Man cannot acquire this learning instantly, but only by gradual steps, in conformity with his nature. To learn in this way he must begin by believing in order that he may eventually arrive at perfect knowledge. . . . Hence for man to attain to the perfect vision of beatitude it is necessary for him first to believe God as a disciple believes the master who teaches him.[14]

Looking upon the content of revelation as something passively received from the mind of God, rather than anything actively discovered by the exercise of reason, Thomas has to face the question how one can recognize authentic divine revelations. On the assumption that the truths of faith are essentially above reason, Thomas cannot admit the possibility of any demonstrative proof of their validity. Hence he holds that they must be confirmed by external signs, especially miracles and prophecies.[15]

In the opening questions of Part 2-2 of the *Summa Theologica,* where Thomas treats of the object of faith, we find his fullest discussion of what we should today call the content of revelation. The formal object of faith, Thomas holds, is "the First Truth insofar as it is divinely revealed" (q. 1, a. 1), or, as he puts it elsewhere, "the First Truth insofar as it is manifested in Holy Scripture and in the doctrine of the Church" (q. 5, a. 3). The material object of faith includes both God and

14. *Summa Theol.* 2–2, q. 2, a. 3 c.
15. *Summa Contra Gentiles,* bk. 3, ch. 154.

the divine actions by which he helps man to come to him. The realities which we believe are known to us through propositions (*enunciabilia*), insofar as the human mind achieves itself by affirming and denying (q. 1, a. 2). The principal contents of faith (*credibilia*) are those set forth in the articles of the creed (q. 1, aa. 6–9).

Following St. Augustine, St. Thomas holds that a divinely infused light is needed to adhere with faith to the revealed truth. But unlike most of the Augustinians, he does not normally use the term "revelation" to designate this interior illumination of the mind inclining it to accept the data of faith. Thus the idea of revelation, in St. Thomas, becomes more objectified than in Augustine and his school.

The historical stages of revelation are described by St. Thomas in several important texts. In one passage,[16] he distinguishes three major stages of public revelation: before the Law, under the Law, and under grace. Revelation before the Law was communicated in the highest degree to its first recipient, Abraham, before whose time such revelation had not been necessary, for men had not yet fallen away from true worship into idolatry. The principal recipient of revelation in its second phase was Moses, and in the time of grace it was communicated in the highest degree to the apostles, to whom the Son of God himself revealed the mystery of the Trinity. Just as the prophets of the Old Testament received further revelations completing that of Moses, but adding nothing essential to it, so in the age of the Church, Christian prophets receive further revelations regarding the ways in which human action should be regulated according to the circumstances of various times. But these revelations add nothing essential to the content of Christian faith.

Prophecy, for St. Thomas, is a species of revelation, excellent in its kind but falling far short of the vision enjoyed by the blessed in heaven (2-2.171.4.ad 2). The charism of prophecy, he maintains, has two facets or moments, called inspiration and revelation. The first connotes the elevation of the mind to a

16. *Summa Theol.* 2–2, q. 174, a. 6.

supernatural plane; the second, the knowledge of divine things resulting from this.[17]

In the course of his treatise on prophecy (2-2.171–178), St. Thomas analyzes with great subtlety the psychology of revelatory experience.[18] Expounding many texts from the Old Testament prophets with the help of the Aristotelian psychology of his day, St. Thomas shows that the intentions and actions of God were disclosed to the ancient seers through a great variety of means, including historical events, symbolic actions, dreams, visions, ecstatic states, and purely intellectual intuitions. In accordance with the primary role which Thomas accords to the judicative element in knowledge, he holds that the formal ingredient in prophetic revelation is the intelligible light that empowers the mind to judge according to the divine truth (q. 173, a. 2).

Finally, in his Christology (*Summa Theologica* 3.1–59), St. Thomas has much to say about the revelatory function of the incarnate Word. Although he looks upon Christ's revelatory work primarily as "teaching," he considers this teaching office concretely, as fulfilled not simply in his verbal discourse, but in his whole visible presence and activity, including the example of his life, his passion, and his resurrection. Thus Thomas does not look upon revelation in merely propositional terms, as some have insinuated.

Thomas's strict distinction between natural knowledge, resting on the inner light of reason, and supernatural knowledge, resting on the infused light of faith, did not go uncontested. Particularly in the Franciscan school, many theologians of the late thirteenth and fourteenth centuries continued to insist that the reasonableness of faith can be known by intrinsic reasons. The enthusiastic Catalan missionary, Ramon Lull (1235?–1316), tried to devise a method of proving all the mysteries of faith by what he called "necessary reasons."

17. *Ibid.,* q. 171, a. 1, ad 4. Cf. Pierre Benoit, *Aspects of Biblical Inspiration* (Chicago, 1965) 50.
18. See the commentary of P. Synave and P. Benoit, *Prophecy and Inspiration* (New York, 1961). Also V. White, *God and the Unconscious* (Cleveland, paperback, 1961) ch. 7.

John Duns Scotus (1265?–1308), although he belonged to the Franciscan order, made much of the distinction between revelation and naturally acquired knowledge. Unlike many medieval theologians, he used the term "revelation" to designate only the original transmission of supernatural truth from God to the "mountains of faith"—that is, the prophets and apostles. Such transmission he held to have occurred thanks to the interior and exterior locutions. The original recipients of revelation, in his view, were given full certitude regarding the contents of revelation, and thus the faith of the Church can securely rest on them. Later Scholasticism was to follow Scotus in his inordinate separation between the initial reception of revelation and the acceptance of revelation as mediated by the Church.

Contrary to Scholasticism was the development that occurred among the followers of the Cistercian Abbot Joachim of Floris (d. 1202), who revived, in their own way, the Montanist idea that the Christian dispensation is not final. The age of the Son was presently coming to an end, they said, to be succeeded by that of the Holy Spirit. The Joachite prophets laid claim to immediate revelations from the Spirit, which they ranked on a par with the biblical oracles. Partly because it unduly separated the work of the Son from that of the Holy Spirit, subordinating the former to the latter, Abbot Joachim's *Eternal Gospel* was condemned by Pope Alexander IV in 1255.

Although the prophecies of Abbot Joachim did not come true, his book did have a certain prophetic significance, which has not escaped the attention of modern philosophers of history. The renowned authority on comparative religion, Mircea Eliade, regards the *Eternal Gospel* as the most significant contribution to the eschatology of history since Augustine's *City of God,* and calls it "a real tragedy for the Western world that Joachim of Floris's prophetico-religious eschatological speculations, though they inspired and fertilized the thought of a St. Francis of Assisi, of a Dante, and of a Savonarola, so quickly sank into oblivion."[19] Linearism and the progressivistic conception of his-

19. Mircea Eliade, *Cosmos and History* (New York, paperback, 1959) 145.

tory did of course reassert themselves in and since the Enlightenment, but in a secularized form which Joachim would have disowned. The contemporary Protestant, Karl Löwith, finds Joachism to blame for having opened the way to the positivistic and materialistic schemes of Comte and Marx, which looked for a fulfilment of history within history itself. "The third dispensation of the Joachites," writes Löwith, "reappeared as a third International and a third *Reich,* inaugurated by a *dux* or a Führer who was acclaimed as a savior and greeted by millions with a *Heil.*"[20]

Two main streams of heresy run through the religious history of medieval Europe. Knox calls them the Waldensian and the Catharist.[21] The Waldensians—named after Peter Waldo, late twelfth century—were evangelical and anti-sacerdotal in tendency, and hence inclined towards "enthusiasm." The Catharists were more interested in doctrine and more radical in their departures from orthodoxy. They taught a dualistic creed, repudiating matter and all that pertained to it (the real Incarnation of the Word, the sacramental system, matrimony, and so forth). Reviving the old Manichaean tenets, they rejected the Old Testament as "carnal." In opposition to this Manichaean-Catharist tendency, the Church repeatedly affirmed that the same God had spoken in the Old Testament and in the New, and had revealed himself progressively in the course of sacred history and, most fully, in the person of Jesus Christ.[22] The Church's stand against the Catharist view of revelation is enunciated most solemnly in the pronouncements of Lateran Council IV (A.D. 1215) (*DS* 800).

On the eve of the Reformation there were many currents of dissatisfaction with official Catholicism. Erasmus, following the Brothers of the Common Life, was calling for a repudiation of Scholastic philosophy and a return to the simplicity of the gospel.

20. Karl Löwith, *Meaning in History* (Chicago, 1949) 159.
21. Ronald Knox, *Enthusiasm: A Chapter in the History of Religion* (New York, 1950) 72.
22. Cf. Denzinger-Schönmetzer, *Enchiridion Symbolorum* (Freiburg im Br., [32]1963) [hereafter abbreviated *DS*] nn. 685, 790, 800, 854, and so forth.

About the same time, enthusiastic movements more or less connected with Waldensianism were breaking out in Holland, Germany, and Switzerland. Shortly after Luther's break with the Church, the Anabaptists of Zwickau advocated the interior guidance of the Holy Spirit, and made much of their own prophetic inspirations. Their dynamic, Spirit-filled doctrine of revelation harks back to the Montanists of the second century and points forward to the Quakers in the seventeenth.

C. The Reformation and the "Age of Orthodoxy"

1. LUTHER

Martin Luther's whole theology is dominated by his own experience of deep religious anguish relieved by a consoling realization of divine forgiveness through the merits of the crucified Christ. Quite naturally, therefore, he develops his doctrine of revelation in the light of his "theology of the Cross."[23] Reason, he insists, cannot attain the true reality of God, and when God reveals himself he can do so only in paradoxical forms, hiding himself under his own opposite. In the crucifixion God proves that he is mighty even in weakness, and thereby manifests his sovereign majesty. In opposition to the spiritual enthusiasts, Luther repeatedly insists that the Holy Spirit never comes to men apart from the word of God.

The "word of God" is for Luther a many-faceted term, which may mean almost anything from the Second Person of the Trinity to the preaching of the Church. Although Luther appealed to the Bible as the sole norm of faith, he did not by any means identify revelation with the letter of the Bible. Rather he understood the Bible in the light of the living Christ, and only in this sense did it become for him the "word of God."

23. On Luther's theology of revelation one may profitably consult Paul Althaus, *The Theology of Martin Luther* (Philadelphia, 1966), part I, "The Knowledge of God"; also P. S. Watson, *Let God Be God!* (London, 1947).

Before Luther felt entitled to use any given biblical text as the "word of God," it had to strike him personally, so that he felt, as we might say today, existentially involved.[24]

Yet there is also a historical aspect to the Bible's value as the word of God. As Professor Pelikan observes: "The Scriptures were the 'Word of God' in a derivative sense for Luther—derivative from the historical sense of the Word as deed and from the basic sense of the Word as proclamation. As a record of the deeds of God, which were the Word of God, the Scriptures participated in the nature of that which they recorded."[25]

In the Bible itself, according to Luther, the word of God comes in two forms. First, as law, it reveals man's sinfulness and condemns him. But then, when one has felt the force of God's wrath, one is disposed for the second form of the word —the gospel which contains God's promise of forgiveness and his bestowal of grace.

In many of his writings Luther dwells on the theme of God as simultaneously hidden and revealed. In his word God reveals himself under alien forms, and thus in a hidden way. Behind this paradoxical revelation lies a hidden and inscrutable God, who retains full freedom to harden and reject those whom he does not choose to vivify with his Spirit.

2. CALVIN

John Calvin (1509–64), who initiated the second great stream of Protestantism, known as the Reformed or Calvinist tradition, was preeminently a theologian of revelation. "Calvin's thought," as E. A. Dowey remarks, "has its whole existence within the realm of God as revealer and man as knower."[26] Book I of Calvin's *Institutes of the Christian Religion* (final edition, 1559) is a systematic treatise on the knowledge of God, both natural

24. Martin Luther, *Über das 1. Buch Mose*, Introduction, WA 24:12.
25. Jaroslav Pelikan, *Luther the Expositor* (St. Louis, 1959) 67.
26. E. A. Dowey, Jr., *The Knowledge of God in Calvin's Theology* (New York, 1952) 3.

and supernatural. Calvin recognizes, in the objective order, a double revelation of God—a natural revelation through the works of creation and a supernatural revelation through the inspired Scriptures. But in the present order, he adds, man never achieves knowledge of God by simple inference from the works of creation. Man's inherited depravity makes him fall into idolatry unless God comes to his help. This God has done through the inspired Scriptures. The Bible is in Calvin's view comparable to a pair of spectacles correcting our faulty vision or to a loud proclamation of that which God has already declared in an ordinary tone of voice through the works of creation.[27] But over and above this naturally knowable content, the Bible gives us certain truths, such as the doctrine of the Trinity, in no way communicated by creation itself.

Calvin insists repeatedly that Scripture teaches everything required for faith and salvation.[28] Hence there is no need to look to tradition, as Catholics do, as a supplementary source, nor to direct revelations of the Spirit, as do the Anabaptists. "Those who, having forsaken Scripture, imagine some way or other of reaching God, ought to be thought of as not so much gripped by error as carried away with frenzy."[29]

On the other hand Calvin makes much of the Holy Spirit as the inner witness that enables us to recognize the Scriptures with certainty as the word of God. While he seeks to maintain an even balance between word and Spirit, as coessential principles, he tends, at least in his later writings, to give primacy to the former. In the judgment of B. A. Gerrish, "For all practical purposes Calvin's final court of appeal is to the letter of the Scripture, and the function of the Spirit is to attest the Scripture *en bloc*."[30]

Calvin's doctrine of revelation, according to Dowey, "concerns itself wholly with the recognition by the believer of the

27. References in Dowey, *op. cit.,* 144.
28. *Ibid.,* 145.
29. *Institutes* I:9:1, Library of Christian Classics, 20 (Philadelphia, 1960) 93.
30. "Biblical Authority and the Continental Reformation," *Scottish Journal of Theology* 10 (1957) 359.

authority of Scripture."[31] This leads, in Dowey's judgment, to a certain incongruity in that Calvin's theory of revelation does not quite tally with his doctrine of faith. For faith, as Calvin sees it, concerns the believer's appropriation not of Scripture, but of Christ. In Calvin's defense, however, one may suggest that his exegesis of Scripture was thoroughly Christocentric. "At the beginning, when the first promise of salvation was given to Adam, it glowed like a feeble spark." Only gradually was the light of revelation diffused until, in the New Testament, "Christ, the Sun of Righteousness, fully illumined the whole earth."[32]

Like Luther, Calvin was first of all a theologian of the "word of God." But in comparison with Luther, Calvin puts greater emphasis on the clarity of God's word rather than on its mysteriousness. He also identifies the word of God more directly with the Bible, which he regards as in some sense verbally inspired. He is less inclined than Luther to play off one biblical text against another—or to appeal from the Bible to Christ—and more given to laborious harmonizations. Further, while agreeing with Luther that revelation comes under the dual form of Law and Gospel, Calvin tends to stress the unity or continuity between the two rather than the dialectical opposition.

3. THE COUNCIL OF TRENT

The Council of Trent, which was convened in 1546 to meet the crisis produced by the Protestant Reformation, in its fourth session (April 8, 1546) promulgated a decree on the measures considered necessary to preserve the "gospel" in its purity. This gospel, which the Council equated with revelation (a term not used in this decree), is described as "the source of all saving doctrine and moral discipline" (*DS* 1501). "Promised of old through the prophets in the sacred Scriptures," it was first promulgated by "our Lord Jesus Christ, Son of God, then

31. *Op. cit.*, 89, note 210.
32. *Institutes* II:10:20.

through his apostles to whom he gave the charge to 'preach it to every creature' (Mk. 16:15)" (*ibid.*). In opposition to the Protestants, the Council defined that the message of the gospel is contained not only in the canonical books of Scripture but also in unwritten traditions, "which have come down to us, having been received by the apostles from the mouth of Christ himself, or from the apostles themselves, by the dictation of the Holy Spirit, have been transmitted, as it were, from hand to hand" (*ibid.*). Although the Council did not specify whether these traditions had any content over and above that of the Bible, it clearly taught that these traditions, "having been preserved by a continual succession in the Catholic Church," were to be received as having an authority equal to that of the Bible itself.

The teaching of Trent in its sixth session (Jan. 13, 1547), regarding the object of justifying faith, is also significant in connection with the theology of revelation. In opposition to extreme fiducial views which were attributed to some Protestants, the Council affirmed that faith involves a free assent to truth elicited with the help of divine grace (*"credentes, vera esse, quae divinitus revelata et promissa sunt,"* DS 1526).

In the wake of the Council of Trent there were long and bitter controversies between Catholics and Protestants on two important questions pertaining to the theology of revelation: the sufficiency or non-sufficiency of Scripture, and the intellectual or fiducial character of faith.

Regarding the first point, Catholic polemicists in the post-Tridentine period argued that without tradition it would be impossible to identify the sacred books or to interpret them correctly; to which the Protestants generally replied that the Bible is self-authenticating (*autopistos*) and self-interpreting (*Scriptura sui ipsius interpres*), at least to those who are docile to the inner witness of the Holy Spirit.

The dispute about the nature of the act of faith was largely a quarrel about words. The Catholics preferred to follow the Scholastic usage, which was influenced by Aristotelian faculty-psychology; the Protestants wished to return to a usage that they considered more biblical (and by this they often meant

Pauline). But behind the question of vocabulary there was also a doctrinal issue. The Protestants, who placed the whole essence of justification in an act by which the believer appropriates to himself the mercy of God extended to him in Christ, could see no value in an act of faith that did not include a trustful self-surrender. The Catholics, on the other hand, while conceding that faith as an intellectual assent was not sufficient for justification, argued that it was nevertheless a gift of God and was salutary insofar as it helped dispose a man for justification.

4. THE AGE OF ORTHODOXY

In the sixteenth and seventeenth centuries, both Protestant and Catholic theology moved in the direction of a new and more rigid Scholasticism. Influenced by the Rationalistic climate of the day, they inordinately intellectualized the notion of revelation. In the Protestant literature of the period, as Emil Brunner has observed,

We search in vain for any comprehensive reflection upon the nature of the revelation upon which the Christian faith is based. . . . Almost without exception "revelation" means the inspiration of Holy Scripture. The statement of the orthodox Lutheran, Calovius, *forma revelationis divinae est theopneustia per quam revelatio divina est quod est,* is not only characteristic of Lutheran orthodoxy, but of the whole of the older theology.[33]

The biblicism of these theologians led them to an almost exclusively propositional view of revelation. As Karl Barth puts it, they looked upon the Bible as "a fixed total of revealed propositions to be systematized like the sections of a *corpus* of law."[34]

The history of the Catholic theology of revelation in this period was no more glorious. The post-Tridentine Scholastics (notably Suárez and de Lugo) shifted the focus of attention

33. *Revelation and Reason* (London, 1947) 7.
34. *Church Dogmatics* I/1 (Edinburgh, 1936) 156.

from revelation understood dynamically as an immediate communication from God to man, to a static and objective view, which looks upon revelation as a commodity already received. The Catholic theologians of the Cartesian and post-Cartesian era, defensively oriented against both the Protestants and the unbelieving Rationalists, were mainly concerned with finding adequate guarantees for their conviction that Scripture and Church tradition really were the word of God. This polemical atmosphere did not favor dispassionate inquiry regarding the nature of revelation itself.

D. Deism

The first full-fledged attack on the traditional Judaeo-Christian notion of revelation was delivered by the Deists. The Dutch Jew, Benedict Spinoza (1632–77), paved the way for this movement by maintaining that reason is solely competent in the sphere of truth; revelation is concerned only with obedience and piety. Theology accordingly must content itself with "defining dogmas of faith only insofar as they may be necessary for obedience, and leaving reason to determine precisely how their truth is to be rationally understood."[35] Revelation, according to Spinoza, can add nothing to what is already knowable by reason, unless it be the assurance that the common man, by simple obedience, can achieve blessedness without philosophical study.

Deism enjoyed great popularity in England in the seventeenth and eighteenth centuries. In essence it was a natural theology based on a mechanistic view of the universe. God was conceived as the manufacturer of the world machine. Some Deists attacked Christianity, others came to its defense. But substantially both parties agreed that Christianity should not seek exemption from the critical norms of reason. Archbishop John Tillotson (1630–94), one of the forerunners of Deism, was orthodox in regarding revelation as a special disclosure of divine

35. *Tractatus Theologico-Politicus*, caput XV, in C. Gebhardt (ed.), Spinoza *Opera* (Heidelberg, 1925), vol. 3, 184.

truths, but these truths, he maintained, were in substance a republication of the law of nature.[36]

John Locke (1632–1704) in his *Essay Concerning Human Understanding* (1700) thus sets forth the relations between reason and revelation:

Reason is natural revelation, whereby the Eternal Father of Light and Fountain of all knowledge, communicates to mankind that portion of the truth which he has laid within the reach of their natural faculties. Revelation is natural reason enlarged by a new set of discoveries communicated by God immediately, which reason vouches the truth of by the testimony and proofs it gives that they come from God.[37]

In explaining what these "new discoveries" are, Locke practically reduces them to things which would be knowable to any wise man, but which escape the understanding of the "illiterate bulk of mankind." He wrote a book, *The Reasonableness of Christianity* (1695), the main object of which, according to Locke himself, was to oppose the rapid spread of Deism.[38] To achieve this end, he sought to show, as B. Willey succinctly declares, "how few and how simple were the credal demands made upon us by Christianity, and how consonant with 'natural revelation' were its moral injunctions."[39]

Locke's admirer, John Toland, who fell away from the Catholicism of his youth, exemplifies the extent to which the Protestantism of his day was sapped by Deistic notions. In his *Christianity Not Mysterious* (1696) he maintained that mysteries have no place in the gospel, for "religion must necessarily be reasonable and intelligible," having come from the Author of

36. For a good summary of Tillotson's views on revelation see H. D. McDonald, *Ideas of Revelation: An Historical Study* A.D. *1700 to* A.D. *1860* (London, 1959) 38–39.

37. *Concerning Human Understanding,* bk. 4, ch. 19, n. 4 (New York, 1947) 340.

38. This is evident from the quotations from Locke's correspondence given in George W. Ewing's introduction to the paperback edition of this work (Chicago, 1965), xii–xiii.

39. B. Willey, *The Seventeenth Century Background* (Garden City, N.Y., 1953) 283.

reason. By definition revelation is clear, for the term itself means the removal of a veil. Mysterious doctrines have crept into Christianity through the foreign influences of Judaism and paganism. The true believer must discard these accretions, restoring the primitive simplicity of the gospel.

Matthew Tindal's *Christianity as Old as the Creation, or the Gospel a Republication of the Religion of Nature* (1730) represents the acme of Deism masquerading as Christianity. Natural religion and revelation, according to Tindal, must perfectly coincide, since the same God is author of both. All that is required for man to know and do is summed up in the Sermon on the Mount. These precepts are all naturally knowable and were, in fact, more clearly stated by Confucius!

The Anglican Bishop Joseph Butler, whose *Analogy of Religion* was published in 1736, sought in his apologetics to go as far as he could with the Deists. He shares their view that "natural religion is the foundation and principal part of Christianity," but, he adds, "it is not in any sense the whole of it."[40] Revelation is not merely a republication of natural religion. It tells us of "somewhat new in the government of the world . . . which could not otherwise have been known."[41] Archdeacon William Paley's *Evidences of Christianity* (1794) likewise makes many compromises with Deistic Rationalism in its arguments on behalf of Christianity. Nearly all the eighteenth-century apologists, as Alan Richardson remarks,[42] misconstrued the meaning of the biblical revelation because they overlooked the historical element in God's salvific action. Revelation could only be, in their estimation, a body of timeless truths.

E. Non-Conformism in England

During the seventeenth and eighteenth centuries the Established Church tried to effect a sort of compromise between Calvinism

40. *The Analogy of Religion,* part II, ch. 1 (New York, 1961) 127.
41. *Ibid.,* 136.
42. Alan Richardson, *The Bible in the Age of Science* (Philadelphia, 1961) 38.

and Catholicism. But Anglicanism was under constant fire from groups who sought to do away with the Catholic remnants. The most vigorous religious movement in seventeenth-century England was Puritanism, a form of Protestantism "marked by an intense experience of the living God, nourished exclusively by the Bible and expressed in every thought and act."[43] Represented by such eminent divines as the Congregationalist John Owen (1616–83) and the Presbyterian Matthew Henry (1662–1714), the Puritans looked to the Bible, as the inspired and infallible word of God, for all religious guidance. But they were intensely logical and systematic in drawing conclusions from Scripture, and their studious Christianity failed to satisfy souls in quest of a warmer and more vital religious existence.

Partly for this reason, seventeenth-century England witnessed a proliferation of enthusiastic sects which became known under such picturesque titles as Ranters, Seekers, Shakers, Quakers, and Creepers. The Quakers, led by George Fox (1624–91), practiced a simple and serious Christianity which avoided the moral excesses of other Enthusiasts. But they modified considerably the traditional Christian notion of revelation. "The fundamental tenet of the Quakers was that God is directly approachable and experienced by men as within themselves. They spoke of the light within, or of Christ within, even of God within. God's spirit was immediately present and discernible to all who sought him in sincerity. His truth and way of life could be directly apprehended. To those Protestants who did not share this conviction, this appeared as a direct denial of everything biblical."[44]

The Evangelicals of the eighteenth century, under the energetic leadership of John Wesley (1703–91), achieved a felicitous compromise between the Puritans' devotion to the Word and the Enthusiasts' cultivation of the Spirit. Wesley was, and wished to be, *homo unius libri*. The Bible was for him "that standing Revelation," inspired and infallible in all its parts. But

43. J. Dillenberger and C. Weich, *Protestant Christianity Interpreted Through Its Development* (New York, 1954) 99.
44. *Ibid.*, 119.

he insisted equally that no genuine Christianity could arise without the illumination of the Spirit—a thought that impelled him to speak of the Montanists as "the real, Scriptural Christians." Revelation therefore comes through a combination of Word and Spirit, Law and Testimony. But his position does not seem to be entirely consistent. Ronald Knox comments: "It seems to be the only possible conclusion that when Wesley talked about 'the Law and the Testimony' he meant his own interpretation of the Bible."[45]

The history of the American colonies exhibits a similar conflict between the formalism of the established Puritan churches and the fervor of the sectaries. The Great Awakenings of the eighteenth century extended to American soil the fruits of English Evangelical Piety.

F. Eighteenth-Century Rationalism

1. LESSING

Eighteenth-century Christianity in continental Europe was heavily influenced by the Deism of the Enlightenment. An excellent specimen of this rationalistic Christianity is offered by the poet, dramatist, and esthete, Gotthold Ephraim Lessing (1729–81), whose program of tolerance is set forth in the celebrated play, *Nathan der Weise*. Son of a Lutheran minister, Lessing was throughout his life concerned with testing his religious heritage by the light of reason. The only true religion, he became convinced, is natural religion—that is, that which lies within the potential range of human reason. In a posthumously published fragment, *On the Origin of Revealed Religion,* he sets forth the principle: "The best revealed or positive religion is that which contains the fewest conventional additions to natural

45. J. Knox, *Enthusiasm* 453–54. A more favorable account of Wesley's doctrine of revelation may be found in H. D. McDonald, *Ideas of Revelation* (cited above), ch. 9.

religion, and least hinders the good effects of natural religion."[46]

Lessing provoked no little scandal by publishing in 1774–77 some fragments from the *Apology for or Defense of the Rational Worshippers of God,* an anti-Christian polemic by the recently deceased Deist, Hermann Samuel Reimarus. But Lessing did not himself share Reimarus' total rejection of revealed religion. He admitted that revelation was true and valuable as a method of educating men in what they had not yet discovered by the diligent use of their own intelligence. "What education is to the individual man, revelation is to the whole human race."[47] It is the divine education of the human race in history. While this educative process is unending, Lessing was ready to recognize that the Christian revelation, purged of its irrational and mysterious ingredients, was the best approximation of the "religion of reason" that man had thus far achieved.

What Lessing did accept from Reimarus was the conviction that Christianity could not effectively be defended by the traditional arguments from the miracles and prophecies recorded in Scripture. Since historical truths themselves could not be demonstrated, he argued, it followed ineluctably that "accidental truths of history can never become the proof of necessary truths of reason."[48] He took it for granted, of course, that religion must deal with eternal and necessary truths.

The best proof of Christianity, according to Lessing, is the knowledge of God we experience when we adhere to it. The ultimate proof, therefore, must be drawn not from history but from personal experience. This Lessing called, in the title of one of his meditations, "the proof of the Spirit and of power" (see 1 Cor. 2:4). The "inner truth" of Christianity, he maintained, consists in "the fact that the revelation speaks directly and with certainty to us ourselves, to our hearts." He himself provisionally accepted the Lutheran confessions on the basis of the fruits encountered in his own experience, but he con-

46. In H. Chadwick (ed.), *Lessing's Theological Writings* (London, 1956) 105.
47. *Ibid.,* 82.
48. *Ibid.,* 53.

ceded that only a comprehensive view of the whole of history (as it would be seen by God) could give final and complete conviction.

Lessing's fragmentary essays on religion exercised a powerful influence on Fichte, Coleridge, and Kierkegaard, and did much to set the stage for the problem of faith and history which is still with us.

2. KANT

Immanuel Kant (1724–1804) shares Lessing's skepticism regarding historical knowledge, and hence regarding the verifiability of any special revelation. But he differs from Lessing by his consciousness of the limits of reason itself. Pure reason, he maintains, cannot establish the existence of transcendent realities. But the ideas of pure speculative reason, such as soul, freedom, and God—unverifiable though they be—are the indispensable basis of morality and religion.

Kant's view on the subject of revelation are most fully set forth in his *Religion Within the Limits of Pure Reason* (1792), in which he maintains that everything sound in religion derives its value from the three postulates of practical reason (immortality, freedom, God)—postulates which provide a valid basis for moral conduct, but do not yield any speculative knowledge about their objects. In the framework of such a philosophic system there is little room for revelation in the traditional Christian sense. Kant respected the Bible to the extent that he could read into it his own philosophical theories. James Collins admirably sums up Kant's views on revelation:

Kant shared the suspicion of the Enlightenment toward positive religion. Historical "revelation" is, at most, a means of communicating the deliverances of practical reason in popular symbolical fashion and with the sanction of external, social authority. The true church is not the external one but the internal one—and it is confined to the rational union of morally upright wills. In effect, this

58

implies the reduction of religion to morality, the religious community to the ethical commonwealth. To be religious means to regard the duties of the moral law as direct divine commands. In his last jottings (gathered together in the *Opus Postumum*), Kant reaffirmed the view that, although God can be approached only through analysis of the needs of practical reason, still he can be found along this route. The religious attitude stresses this positive aspect of our practical life, and hence treats conscience as though it were the intimate voice of God. What religion supplies is not an immediate divine revelation, but a way of treating the moral imperative as if it were such a revelation. The moral law and God are made as one, in the view of rational, moral religion. Fichte will simply remove these qualifications and make an outright identification of God with the immanent moral law.[49]

Kant's system, then, does not allow for any revelation of the Transcendent to speculative or theoretical reason, man's power of reflecting on the data presented to him by experience. Kant's ethic is independent of any prior metaphysic. But, as he asserts in his *Foundations of a Metaphysics of Morals,* practical reason, in its response to the sense of moral obligation, opens the way for religious faith. If a man is able to believe that he can share in an eternal purpose under the guidance of a divine leader, he will be able to conform his conduct more easily to the demands of the categorical imperative. Thus the precepts of the practical reason are virtually equivalent to a divine revelation.

3. FICHTE

Kant's immediate disciple Johann Gottlieb Fichte (1762–1814) made his reputation by an early *Essay Towards a Critique of All Revelation* (1792), in which he carefully applied Kant's critical principles to the question of revealed religion. His mature philosophy of religion is set forth in his *The Way to the Blessed Life or Doctrine of Religion* (1806), in which he "measures Christianity and all religious life according to the standard of

49. James Collins, *A History of Modern European Philosophy* (Milwaukee, 1954) 534.

his own philosophical idealism."[50] He propounds the typically idealistic position that Jesus deserves to be called "the only-begotten and first-begotten Son of God" because he brought to mankind the "miraculous" insight of the "absolute unity of human existence with the Divine Existence." Once union with God has been achieved through discovering this doctrine, man has no further dependence on the mediation of Jesus. "If a man is really united to God, and has entered into Him, it matters not at all by which way he came to Him and it would be a very profitless and perverse occupation if instead of living the reality, we were continually to repeat the memory of the way to it."[51] Fichte's dictum, "only the metaphysical can save, never the historical," reflects the profound influence of Lessing upon him.

4. COLERIDGE

The poet and essayist, Samuel Taylor Coleridge (1772–1834), was largely responsible for introducing the new currents of German Idealism into British theology. On the basis of a Subjective Idealism resembling that of Fichte he maintained that religion was the welling up of the divine within. His view of revelation, expressed in the following passage, is strangely premonitory of Tillich:

Revealed religion (and I know of no religion not revealed) is in its highest contemplation the unity, that is, the identity or coinherence, of Subjective and Objective. It is in itself, and irrelatively, at once inward Life and Truth, and outward Fact and Luminary. But as all Power manifests itself in the harmony of correspondent Opposites, each supposing and supporting the other,—so has Religion its objective, or historic and ecclesiastical pole, and its subjective, or spiritual and individual pole. In the miracles, and miraculous parts of religion—both in the first communication of divine truths, and in the promulgation of the truths thus communicated—we have the

50. *Ibid,* 568.
51. Quoted by Paul Althaus, *The So-Called Kerygma and the Historical Jesus* (London, 1959) 13–14.

union of the two, that is, the subjective and supernatural displayed objectively—outwardly and phenomenally—*as* subjective and supernatural.[52]

In his *Confessions of an Inquiring Spirit* Coleridge devotes himself assiduously to the problem of determining the bounds "between the right, and the superstitious, use and estimation of the Sacred Canon." While holding to divine inspiration, he follows Lessing by rejecting "bibliolatry," or the simple identification of revelation with the letter of holy Writ.

Coleridge himself was too eclectic and fragmentary a writer to be ranked among the theologians, but he did exert considerable influence on what came to be called the Broad Church. F. D. Maurice, in his *What Is Revelation?* (published 1859) develops the Coleridgean idea that the Bible is to be accepted, not because it contains infallible propositional truth, but because one can hear within it Christ speaking to him in his very heart. Maurice is in many ways close to Schleiermacher, whose work he defended in England. To Schleiermacher, therefore, we must now turn our attention.

52. *Confessions of an Inquiring Spirit* (Stanford, Calif., 1957) 79.

61

3. THE NINETEENTH CENTURY

The nineteenth century presents an extremely rich development of the theology of revelation under the stimulating impact of idealistic philosophy on the one hand and of historical thinking on the other. Idealistic philosophy, rebelling against the narrowness of eighteenth-century Rationalism, rediscovered the Absolute in a new way. Historical thinking, on the contrary, made theologians conscious of the cultural relativity of their ideas about God.

A. Theologies of Feeling and Subjectivity

1. SCHLEIERMACHER

Like Tillich in our own century, Friedrich D. E. Schleiermacher (1768–1834) aimed to be a mediator among mutually opposed groups. Raised in an atmosphere of Pietism, he became a disciple of Kant and later an admirer of Plato. He moved in a circle of German Romantics, and for their benefit wrote an early series of *Speeches on Religion to Its Cultured Despisers* (1799). His masterpiece is a profound systematic work, *The Christian Faith* (first edition, 1821–22), perhaps the greatest Protestant dogmatic synthesis since Calvin's *Institutes*.

Following up certain suggestions in the Kantian "Critiques," Schleiermacher based his philosophy of religion not upon speculative reason but upon the sentiments of the heart (though his term, *Gefühl*, might almost be translated "intuition" as opposed to abstractive thinking). His cardinal principle is that man in experiencing flux and contingency acquires an interior feeling of his own total dependence on the changeless, the necessary, the infinite. This feeling of absolute dependence Schleiermacher defines as religion. It gives rise to the idea of God. Revelation interests Schleiermacher not insofar as it is a free intervention of God breaking into the world from outside, but rather as an unexpected transformation in man's religious consciousness. "Every original communication of the Universe to man is revelation."[1] "The idea of revelation signifies the *originality* of the fact which lies at the foundation of a religious communion" —a fact which cannot be simply explained by the historical chain that preceded it.[2]

Not only Christianity, but all religious movements rest upon some distinctive insight, and are in that sense revealed. But the Christian religion rests upon the unique God-consciousness of Christ, who was so closely united to God that he needed no other mediator, whereas other mediators can mediate the Christ-experience.[3] To be a Christian is to belong to the historical communion of those who share in the mind and life of Christ (the Holy Spirit).

Schleiermacher made a radical departure from the heavy emphasis on doctrine which had been dominant in Protestantism since the seventeenth century. For him, as has been said, "The content of revelation is not dogma or doctrine, or the raw material of dogma or doctrine, but 'immediate awareness'; and in its substance theology is man's expression of, and commentary on, this consciousness or awareness of God."[4] Schleiermacher's intuitional or experiential approach to theology was welcomed by many Christians of his age, who found in it an aid to piety at a time when Kantian criticism was making it difficult to venture forth on the high seas of orthodoxy.

After Feuerbach and Freud had made their devastating critique of religion, theologians such as Karl Barth and Emil

1. *On Religion* (New York, paperback, 1958) 89.
2. *The Christian Faith* 1 (New York, paperback, 1963) 50.
3. Cf. *On Religion*, 247.
4. R. C. Johnson, *Authority in Protestant Theology* (Philadelphia, 1959) 74.

Brunner began to seek a standpoint quite different from Schleiermacher's. But Barth, one of the sharpest critics of Schleiermacher's anthropocentrism, pays him this tribute:

The first place in a history of the theology of the most recent times belongs and will always belong to Schleiermacher, and he has no rival. . . . Nobody can say today whether we have really overcome his influence, or whether we are still at heart children of his age, for all the protest against him, which now, admittedly, has increased in volume and is carried out according to his basic principles.[5]

The protest to which Barth here alludes was led, in great part, by Barth himself. In the past decade, theologians who shy away from Barth's own dogmatic supernaturalism have begun to study Schleiermacher with renewed interest and respect.

2. SCHELLING

Friedrich Wilhelm Joseph Schelling (1775–1854) received his early training at the Tübingen theological foundation, where Hegel was one of his classmates. While still at Tübingen, he became so adept at expounding Fichte that he was known as "the second founder of the theory of science." Like Schleiermacher, he associated with Romantic leaders, such as Hölderlin, Novalis, and the Schlegels, and made ample room for art and intuition in his philosophy. In later years he became critical of Hegel on the ground that the latter's logical method, while valid in the spheres of possibility and general essences, was incompetent to deal with freedom, history, and actual existence.

Schelling's religious philosophy is set forth in his *Philosophy and Religion* (1804) and in two important posthumous works, *Philosophy of Revelation* and *Introduction to the Philosophy of Mythology*. These works manifest the influence of the Renaissance pantheist Giordano Bruno and of the seventeenth-century mystic and theosophist, Jacob Boehme. Notwithstanding his

5. K. Barth, *Protestant Theology From Rousseau to Ritschl* (New York, 1959) 306–307.

pantheistic tendencies, Schelling regards God as "Lord of history" and makes room for revelation as a free intervention of God in the world. While looking on the whole history of the religious consciousness as God's revelation of himself, Schelling describes Christianity as the culmination of historical religion and in this sense as "specially" revealed.

3. KIERKEGAARD

The Danish philosopher Søren Kierkegaard (1813–55), who attended Schelling's lectures at Berlin in 1841, received with great enthusiasm Schelling's contention that a system such as Hegel's, being based primarily on concepts and essences, is unsuited to deal either with the divine existence or with the contingencies of human history. Convinced that the efforts of orthodox Christians to bolster their religion by the principles of Hegelian dialectics were futile and impious, Kierkegaard launched satirical invectives against the reigning philosophy of his day. The truths of revelation, he maintained, are existential; they belong to the order of real becoming, freedom, history, and individual striving. Accepting Lessing's premise that "accidental historical truths can never serve as proofs for the eternal truths of reason," Kierkegaard added that "the transition by which it is proposed to base an eternal truth upon historical testimony is a leap."[6] The Christian revelation, being sheer paradox, cannot be made plausible on philosophic or scientific grounds; it demands the existential commitment of blind faith. "The man called by a revelation, to whom was entrusted a doctrine, argues from the fact that this was a revelation, from the fact that he has authority. . . . Authority is the qualitatively decisive point."[7]

Since man is utterly unlike God, reason cannot, of itself, bridge the gap. But God can humble himself and come to man. Revelation, for Kierkegaard, is necessarily authoritative, para-

6. *Concluding Unscientific Postscript* (Princeton, 1941) 86.
7. *On Authority and Revelation* (Princeton, 1955) 107.

doxical, offensive to reason. Yet it is not totally unassimilable, because "Reason, in its paradoxical passion, precisely desires its own downfall. But this is what the Paradox also desires, and thus they are at bottom linked in understanding, but this understanding is present only in the moment of passion."[8]

Kierkegaard draws a sharp contrast between Socratic learning, which aims to grasp the content of the teaching by setting the teacher aside, and revelation, which demands personal adherence to the teacher himself. In the Socratic order, the learner is self-possessed and the teacher is ultimately dispensable. But in faith the disciple owes everything, including his very capacity to assent, to the teacher. For the object of faith is the Paradox of the Eternal made historical. Neither reason nor volition is capable of the act of faith, for the underlying conditions of such self-transcendence are not present within man. Faith presupposes the miracle whereby the eternal condition is given in time.[9]

Kierkegaard's existential reply to the reigning rationalistic Idealism was so alien to the spirit of his age that he was almost ignored until he was rediscovered by the Dialectical Theologians in the period following World War I. After a generation of popularity, Kierkegaard seems to be passing behind a cloud once again. Many feel that his insistence on authority, paradox, and uniqueness was so extreme as to deprive faith of its meaning as well as of its rationality.

B. Hegelian Idealism

1. HEGEL

Although primarily famed as a philosopher, Georg W. F. Hegel (1770–1831) was so concerned with theological questions and exercised so great an influence on subsequent theology that the elements of his system must be known. Seeking to over-

8. *Philosophical Fragments* (Princeton, [2]1962) 59.
9. *Ibid.*, 73–81.

come the metaphysical agnosticism of Kant, he held that noumenal reality was a continuously evolving process, passing through the triadic phases of thesis, antithesis, and synthesis. Absolute Spirit (God) was in his system the ultimate term of all progress. It manifests itself historically by the emergence of three great cultural phenomena: art, religion, and philosophy. *Art* (thesis) grasps the Absolute Spirit in concrete, sensuous intuitions, at the imaginative level. In *religion* (antithesis), mind perceives its own superiority to the particularized images of finite thing, and relates itself to the infinite. But religion is still bound to symbolic representations as the media by which it is aroused and expressed. In *philosophy* (synthesis), the mind transcends all these symbols and attains the Absolute in its own reality, under the form of rational concepts.

Hegel professed singular devotion to Christianity, in its Protestant and Lutheran form, as the ultimate and highest embodiment of the religious consciousness. So far as content goes, the Christian dogmas were for him unsurpassably true, and in a certain sense "revealed."[10] Revealed religion, however, is defective insofar as it fails to attain the Absolute except under the form of obscure symbolism, by an imaginative type of thinking (*Vorstellung*). It must therefore be eventually supplanted by philosophy.

Hegel respected and sought to do justice to the historical factor in Christianity, but at the same time he denied that this had the absolute worth which theologians attributed to it. For Hegel the historical factor would ultimately be sublated in philosophical speculation and man would escape from the relativities of temporal process. Thus philosophical reason in his system takes the place of the parousia in orthodox Christianity.

Hegel attempted to fit the Christian concept of revelation into his system, but could not do so without considerable violence. Revelation was for him the provisional (pre-philosophical) self-manifestation of the Absolute Spirit in history. It was not

10. J. Collins, *A History of Modern European Philosophy* (Milwaukee, 1954) 653.

the free intervention of an eternally existent God, but the necessary self-generation of Absolute Spirit through the dialectic of historical process. In Hegel's thinking faith is totally subordinated to reason, and religion to philosophy.

2. HEGELIANS OF THE NINETEENTH CENTURY

Theologians who accepted the general principles of Hegelian Idealism became divided almost from the start into two camps —those of the right who held that the historical Jesus of Nazareth was the total and exclusive embodiment of the God-man unity, and those of the left who departed in various ways and degrees from orthodox, Chalcedonian Christology, if not from the whole Christian idea of God.

The stalwarts of the right wing (Göschel, Gabler, Marheinecke, and others) have passed into near oblivion and need not be discussed here.

An independent Hegelian who belongs more to the "left" than to the "right," though not precisely identifiable with either, was Ferdinand Christian Baur (1792–1860), whom Wilhelm Dilthey was to praise as the greatest theologian of the century. Setting out from Hegel's monistic pantheism, Baur regarded the entire process of history as revelation, in the sense that it was a function of divine life explicitating itself outwardly. This revelatory process, he maintained, had reached its high point in Christ, who was the highest possible—and yet not the absolutely perfect—historical embodiment of the idea of divine-human reconciliation. With his deep respect for history, Baur accused both Schleiermacher and Hegel of a new Gnosticism, in which the positive content of historical Christianity was absorbed into a general idea. In his own theology he engaged in painstaking historical-critical research, which he regarded as a deeply religious task and a necessary means of discovering what God has to say to us through history. Baur is of lasting significance because, as Peter Hodgson has pointed out, he contributed mightily to the foundation of the new discipline of "historical-critical theology." Seeking to give their due to the subjective commitment of faith and to the objective demands of scientific scholarship, he refused to sacrifice either to the other.[11]

David Friedrich Strauss (1808–74), a more radical member of the Hegelian "left," is notable for his application of Hegelian principles to the historical criticism of the gospels. Holding that the essence of the Christian faith consisted in the emergence of the supremely valid idea of humanity's oneness with God, he believed it possible to engage in a thoroughly destructive critical study of the life of Jesus without undermining the essential veracity of the Christian message. But, as Miegge points out,[12] Strauss was far more concerned than most of the Hegelians with the gospel narratives. His exposure of what he regarded as legend, myth, and fable in the New Testament is closer to the spirit of Reimarus and the Enlightenment than to Hegel. But he differed from both Reimarus and Hegel insofar as he believed that the truth of religion is not rational or philosophical, but mythical.

Among the most extreme members of the Hegelian "left" was Ludwig Feuerbach (1804–72), who maintained that the idea of God was a human projection, representing the "antithesis" of man's own defects. This projection, he believed, had outlived its usefulness and must now be replaced by the idea of a "divinized humanity," synthesizing the attributes of God and man, so that the religion of man might replace that of the transcendent God.

C. Trends in Nineteenth-Century Catholicism

Under the prodding of Rationalism and Idealism in their various forms, Catholic theology began to reawaken from the dogmatic slumbers to which it had succumbed since the Counter Reforma-

11. Cf. P. C. Hodgson, *The Formation of Historical Theology: A Study of F. C. Baur* (New York, 1966).

12. G. Miegge, *Gospel and Myth in the Thought of Rudolf Bultmann* (London, 1960) 112–13.

tion and to grapple anew with the problem of revelation. Speculatively minded theologians tried to see to what extent they could appropriate the insights of their Protestant colleagues.

1. SEMI-RATIONALISM

Semi-Rationalism may be regarded as an incursion into Catholic theology of the epistemologies of various Rationalists from Descartes to Hegel. Unlike many Hegelians, the Semi-Rationalists were sincere believers who accepted the Christian revelation as definitively valid. They maintained, however, that reason could demonstrate by intrinsic arguments all the truths of revelation.

Georg Hermes (1775–1831), a theology professor at Münster and Bonn, applied to faith the principles of Cartesian doubt. Having called everything into question, he sought to reestablish from reason what he had previously believed as a matter of faith. Revelation was in his view the mode of knowledge which the ignorant should practice owing to their incapacity to discern the truth about God through scientific demonstration; but the wise, he thought, could substitute clear philosophic knowledge for the obscurity of faith. Even for the wise, grace would still be necessary to bring about the total submission of their lives to the truths of revelation. Hermes' doctrine, very popular in his own lifetime, was not condemned until after his death.[13]

Anton Günther (1783–1863), an Austrian priest, was convinced that Scholasticism was outmoded by Kantian criticism and that theology must seek a new philosophical basis. His own system owed much to Descartes, Hegel, and Schelling. With regard to revelation, his position hardly differs from that of Hermes. On the ground that human reason was omnicompetent, he denied that revelation could be absolutely necessary to manifest any truth whatever. Theological progress in his view con-

13. Cf. the Brief of Gregory XVI, *Dum acerbissimas*, Sept. 26, 1835 (*DS* 2738–40).

sisted in a reduction of faith to rational knowledge through a deeper understanding of the divinely attested truth. Günther's writings were placed on the Index in 1857,[14] and he immediately submitted.

Jacob Frohschammer (1821–93), a professor at Munich, wrote various books that were placed on the Index in 1857. He never submitted, but he continued to profess the Catholic faith until his death. A more moderate Semi-Rationalist than Hermes or Günther, he held that *pure* reason could never comprehend the mysteries of revelation. But he added that reason as intrinsically modified and developed under the influence of Christian revelation could do so. The phrase, *"humana ratio historice exculta,"* which appears in certain Roman documents,[15] is an allusion to this tenet of Frohschammer's.

2. FIDEISM AND TRADITIONALISM

Fideism, which had been somewhat characteristic of much Protestant thinking from Luther to Kierkegaard, came into Catholic theology under the influence of Kantian agnosticism and the general climate of ideas at the time of the Romantic revival (Schleiermacher, Schelling). In extreme opposition to the Rationalists, the Fideists unduly depressed the powers of human reason. They maintained that supernatural faith was absolutely required in order for man to perceive fundamental truths of a religious nature, such as the existence and attributes of God, the immortality of the soul, the precepts of the moral law, and, more generally, all that Thomistic theology designated as "preambles of faith."

Catholic fideism is principally associated with the name of Abbé Louis M. E. Bautain (1796–1867), an exemplary Alsatian priest filled with zeal for the restoration of "Christian philosophy." Partly because he failed to express himself in the

14. Cf. the Brief of Pius IX, *Eximiam tuam,* June 15, 1857 (*DS* 2828–31).

15. Pius IX, *Syllabus of Errors,* n. 9 (*DS* 2909); cf. *DS* 2878 and *DS* 3041.

standard terminology of the Roman school, he was removed from his post as seminary director and on various occasions compelled to sign lists of propositions drawn up respectively by his local ordinary and by the Sacred Congregation of Bishops and Regulars.[16] These propositions have very little dogmatic weight, and contain some theologically unfortunate expressions.[17]

Traditionalism may be regarded as a particular form of Fideism. Making a sharp distinction between general and special revelation, the Traditionalists maintained that to know any truths of the suprasensible order, man needed at least a general revelation. God had made such a revelation at the beginning of time, and this primitive revelation was passed down through oral tradition. Human society as a whole was the vehicle of this religious tradition, and thus constituted the organ of general revelation. The common consent of the human race was the primary criterion of certitude in moral and religious matters. Traditionalism in the strict sense was most prominently represented by the Vicomte Louis G. A. de Bonald (1754–1840) and his more radical disciple Abbé Félicité de Lammenais (1782–1854). The work of the latter was condemned by Gregory XVI in 1834.[18] A more moderate form of Traditionalism, subsequently excogitated by Augustin Bonnetty (1798–1879), was likewise condemned for undermining the importance of human reason in preparing the way for faith.[19] According to moderate Traditionalism, human reason was not entirely powerless in the realm of religious truths, but it was at least morally incapable of discovering some of the most important of them, such as the attributes of God and the final destiny of man.

16. Cf. *DS* 2751–56 and *DS* 2765–69.
17. See the judicious comments of Roger Aubert in *Le problème de l' acte de foi* (Louvain, [2]1950) 120–21.
18. The pertinent sections of Gregory XVI's encyclical, *Singulari nos,* may be found in Denzinger-Bannwart, *Enchiridion Symbolorum* ([30]1955) n. 1617. They are not reproduced in *DS*.
19. Cf. the theses of the Congregation of the Index, June 1855, *DS* 2811–14.

As we shall presently see, Vatican Council I[20] condemned Traditionalism in the strict sense, insofar as this doctrine would deny the capacity of the human mind to acquire any valid knowledge of divine things without the help of revelation. The magisterium, however, has never denied the de facto existence and transmission of a general revelation. The Traditionalist doctrine of primitive revelation is no longer defended in our day,[21] but the movement has some interesting points of similarity with the theory of "linguisticality" proposed by the later Heidegger and some of his theological disciples.[22]

3. ORTHODOX CATHOLIC THEOLOGIANS

The pillars of Catholic orthodoxy in the nineteenth century were the Jesuits of the Roman College (Gregorian University). The names of Giovanni Perrone (1794–1876) and Johannes Baptist Franzelin (1816–86) are especially worthy of note. Perrone was outstanding as an apologist. Franzelin, who made an important contribution to Vatican Council I, constructed his theology of revelation out of elements borrowed from Suárez and de Lugo.

The most creative Catholic theologians of the century were critical of the excessively arid types of Scholasticism that had become standard in the seminaries. Three theologians may be specially mentioned for their contributions to the theology of revelation.

Johann Adam Möhler (1796–1838) learned from his great teacher at Tübingen, Johann Sebastian Drey, to look upon revelation not as a static body of timeless truths but as God's

20. *DS* 3004, 3036; see below, p. 76.
21. Cf. J. Daniélou, *God and the Ways of Knowing* (New York, 1957) 17. J. R. Geiselmann, while separating himself from strict Traditionalism, with its tenet that man first acquires knowledge of God through an authoritative revelation, makes much of the importance of immemorial tradition in religion. Cf. his *The Meaning of Tradition* (*Quaestiones Disputatae* 15) (New York, 1966) 81–97.
22. See below, pp. 126–28.

dynamic self-manifestation through his actual deeds in history, culminating in the Incarnation. Möhler, especially in his earlier works, stressed the dynamic role of the Holy Spirit in terms reminiscent of Schleiermacher. In 1832 he wrote his *Symbolik*, a work contrasting the objective purity of Catholic doctrine with the confused subjectivism of the Protestants. This involved him in a controversy with his Tübingen colleague F. C. Baur.

John Henry Newman (1801–90), the great antagonist of theological Liberalism, was chiefly preoccupied with the dogmatic and authoritative character of revelation. In opposition to the prevalent Rationalism he insisted on the mysteriousness of the revealed dogmas:

No Revelation can be complete and systematic, from the weakness of the human intellect; so far as it is not such, it is mysterious. When nothing is revealed, nothing is known, and there is nothing to contemplate or marvel at; but where something is revealed, and only something, for all cannot be, there are forthwith difficulties and perplexities. A Revelation is religious doctrine viewed on its illuminated side; a mystery is the selfsame doctrine viewed on the side unilluminated.[23]

Thanks to his perception of the limits of the intellect, the importance of living experiential knowledge, and the historically conditioned nature of all dogmatic formulations, Newman became one of the major contributors to the theology of the future.[24]

Matthias Joseph Scheeben (1835–88) developed the Catholic doctrine of mystery in opposition to the Rationalists and Semi-Rationalists. He likewise contributed to the Trinitarian understanding of revelation. According to his view, revelation always occurs through the Son as Logos, but its acceptance requires an interior enlightenment of the Holy Spirit, which likewise deserves to be called revelation.

23. From Tract 73; excerpt in V. F. Blehl, *The Essential Newman* (New York, paperback, 1963) 100.
24. Newman's contribution is ably assessed by E. Schillebeeckx, *Revelation and Theology* 1 (New York, 1967) 68–71.

4. THE SYLLABUS OF ERRORS: VATICAN COUNCIL I

Less than a decade before the First Vatican Council, Pius IX in his *Syllabus of Errors* (1864) summarized a number of earlier condemnations. In its section on Rationalism this document reasserted the sovereign normative value of revelation (*DS* 2904), its inability to be increased through the mere development of man's rational life (*DS* 2905), its harmony with the deliverances of reason (*DS* 2906), and, in opposition to scholars such as Strauss, the historical validity of the biblical prophecies and miracles (*DS* 2907). The following section, on Semi-Rationalism, denies that human reason, even when historically educated, could demonstrate all the Christian dogmas (*DS* 2909).

Vatican Council I came closer than any previous Church Council to setting forth an authoritative Catholic view of revelation. In its third session (April 24, 1870) it adopted the Dogmatic Constitution *Dei Filius* on Catholic Faith, which on the whole reaffirms the main positions of St. Thomas on revelation insofar as these had become the common property of the post-Tridentine Scholastic tradition.

In opposition to the Rationalists and Hegelians, the Council insisted strongly on the possibility and knowability of strictly supernatural revelation. With regard to religious knowledge, the Council made a sharp distinction between the two orders, natural and supernatural (*DS* 3004). Revelation is defined primarily in terms of this dichotomy: it is supernaturally communicated knowledge. The Council emphasizes the gratuity of revelation (*ibid.*) and its absolute necessity if man is to attain eternal salvation (*DS* 3005). For the attainment of a naturally possible knowledge of the divine, moreover, revelation is said to be morally necessary, in the sense that without it the majority of men would not be able to achieve a suitable knowledge of religious matters with facility, certitude, and accuracy (*DS* 3005, with footnote reference to St. Thomas).

In opposition to the Semi-Rationalists, Vatican Council I

75

insists that the contents of revelation are to be accepted on the authority of the revealing God, and by the help of his grace, rather than on the basis of intrinsic evidence (*DS* 3008). Revelation includes certain strict mysteries, which remain veiled even after revelation, and can in no way be known by merely rational investigation (*DS* 3016, 3041). On the other hand, it is possible for human reason to attain a measure of understanding of what has been revealed, thanks to the inner coherence of revelation itself, its analogy with things naturally knowable, and its harmony with man's dynamism toward his last end (*DS* 3016). Against the Fideists, the Council asserts that the assent of faith is not a blind impulse of the soul, but a fully reasonable act. The credibility of the Christian revelation is sufficiently evidenced by miracles, prophecies, and the standing miracle of the Church itself (*DS* 3009–14). The Council singles out for special reprobation the view (that of Günther already noted) that Catholics may have a just cause to retract their assent of faith until they had achieved a scientific demonstration of credibility (*DS* 3036).

Against the idea that revelation is something progressively discovered by human effort, the Council declared that it is a "divine deposit delivered to the Spouse of Christ, to be faithfully kept and infallibly declared" (*DS* 3020). The notion of the "deposit" is further clarified in connection with the definition of papal infallibility. "For the Holy Spirit was not promised to the successors of Peter that by his revelation they might make known new doctrine, but that by His assistance they might inviolably keep and faithfully expound the revelation or deposit of faith delivered through the apostles" (*DS* 3070). In the same context the Council touched on the universality of the Christian revelation: "that the salutary doctrine of Christ might be propagated among all nations of the earth . . ." (*ibid.*).

Did Vatican Council I espouse a propositional view of revelation? The charge has been made, but is not wholly true. With reference to the object of revelation the Council states that it pleased God "to reveal Himself and the eternal decrees of his will" (*DS* 3004), rather than a set of propositions about himself. Nevertheless the Council evidently looks upon revelation in its finished form as word, that is, "*verbum Dei scriptum vel traditum*" (*DS* 3011). The deeds of God ("*facta divina*") are mentioned (*DS* 3009), but only as extrinsic signs authenticating the words of those who speak in the name of God. In giving a fuller role to revelation through events, Vatican II was to progress beyond Vatican I.

The doctrine of Vatican I must be understood against the background of its times. The Constitution *De Fide Catholica* is intended less as a positive and balanced expression of the nature of revelation than as the answer of a beleaguered Church to certain philosophical and theological systems deemed incompatible with the Church's dogmatic heritage. In comparison with the more concrete and historical point of view of Trent and some earlier Councils, Vatican I looks upon revelation from an abstract and almost metaphysical point of view. Its teaching has remarkable conceptual clarity but lacks the biblical and existential tone which Vatican II sought to restore.

D. Liberal Protestantism

1. RITSCHL

A student under F. C. Baur, Albrecht Ritschl (1822–89) was nurtured in the pure Hegelianism of the school of Tübingen. But he reacted in the direction of Kantian moralism and positivism, and became more conservative than his masters in his evaluation of historic Christianity.[25]

Central to Ritschl's system is the dichotomy between speculative judgments (*Seinsurteile*) and value judgments (*Werturteile*). Science deals with the former, religion with the latter.

25. For a recent critical survey of Ritschl's views on theology and history see Philip Hefner, *Faith and the Vitalities of History* (New York, 1966).

Value judgments do not attempt to pronounce on things as they are in themselves, but as they are for us. Their truth is practical, not theoretical. Ritschl's distinction between these two types of judgment obviously depends on Kant, but it also goes back, in some respects, to the way of apprehending Christ characteristic of the early Luther and of Melanchthon. One thinks in this connection of the latter's famous words: "To know Christ is to know his benefits, not . . . to contemplate his natures" (*Loci Communes,* 1521).

The distinctive feature of Christianity, according to Ritschl, is that it identifies God as love—that is, as him who forgives our sins, removes our natural limitations, admits us to his Kingdom, and makes us his children. All of this is accomplished through Christ. Because Christ is the archetypal idea of the humanity which is to be united in the Kingdom of God, and his whole function is to manifest the God of love, we can say that for us Christ has the value of God. In this sense Ritschl subscribes to the Pauline formula, "God was truly in Christ" (2 Cor. 5:19).

Ritschl and his disciples were the sworn enemies of all dogmatism, which for them represented a confusion between speculative and practical thinking and a Hellenization of the gospel. They sought to get behind Greek speculation and recover the simple message of Jesus. This was presumed to consist essentially in the doctrine of the Kingdom of God, which in turn was interpreted as an invisible union among all men who are loyal to God's will. The Ritschlians esteemed the Synoptic Gospels—especially Mark and the hypothetical "Q" document—as historically reliable sources from which it was possible to recover the authentic teaching of Jesus himself.

Ritschl and his followers still made use of the concept of revelation, but only in a changed sense. For them it was no longer a supernatural communication of truth to be believed, but the manifestation of an ideal that enabled man to escape from his normal limitations and to realize the immanent aspirations of his spiritual nature.

78

2. HERRMANN

The greatest pure theologian of the Ritschlian school, according to D. M. Baillie, was Wilhelm Herrmann of Marburg (1846–1922). For Herrmann the starting point of Christian faith must never be an abstract dogmatic formulation about Christ, but the historical Jesus given to us in the Gospels. "We know only one fact in the whole world," wrote Herrmann,[26] "which can give us the full certainty that God exists for us, . . . namely the appearance of Jesus in history." For Herrmann the revelation given in Christ has two sides to it—the positive historical datum of Jesus of Nazareth, *and* the practical reason by which we recognize this datum as possessing that kind of ultimate moral demand which makes God-language appropriate. The positive datum, moreover, is not so much mere biographical information about Jesus as rather the "inner life" of Jesus which is supposed to make an "impression" (*Eindruck* —to be understood in the strong sense like the impression on a coin) on the mind of the disciple. The inner life of Jesus, as portrayed in the gospel story, exhibits and communicates the power of omnipotent Goodness. According to Herrmann:

All revelation is the self-revelation of God. We can call any sort of communication revelation only then, if we have found God in it. But we find and have God only when he so incontestably touches and seizes us that we wholly yield ourselves to him. . . . God reveals himself in that he forces us to trust him wholly.[27]

Though Herrmann's pietism and his oversimplification of the problem of the historical Jesus make him a child of his time, he still continues to exercise a powerful influence, partly through his immediate pupils Barth and Bultmann, and partly through

26. *The Communion of the Christian with God* ([1]ET) 52; quoted by D. C. Macintosh, *The Problem of Religious Knowledge* (New York, 1940) 258.
27. *Der Begriff der Offenbarung* (1887) 11; quoted by H. R. Niebuhr, *The Meaning of Revelation* (New York, paperback, 1967) 111.

the careful attention given to his work by post-Bultmannians such as Gerhard Ebeling and James M. Robinson. The "new quest" of the historical Jesus in some ways approximates the experiential theology of Herrmann.

3. HARNACK

The most famous of the Ritschlians is the Berlin professor, Adolf von Harnack (1851–1930), who wrote with extraordinary learning on the origins of the gospels and the history of dogma in the ancient Church. But all his scholarship was dedicated to the cause of supporting his own Ritschlian concept of *Christianity*. His *Das Wesen des Christentums* (1900; ET, *What Is Christianity?*, 1901) was an effort to separate the kernel of the original gospel from the husk of traditional teaching. "The Gospel in the Gospel," he contended, "is something so simple, something that speaks to us with so much power, that it cannot be easily mistaken."[28] While shrinking from any dogmatic affirmations about who Jesus was, Harnack found in the gospel a kind of divine revelation in the Ritschlian sense. "No one who accepts the Gospel, and tries to understand him who gave it to us, can fail to affirm that here the divine appeared in as pure a form as it can appear on earth, and to feel that for those who followed him Jesus was himself the strength of the Gospel."[29]

Ritschlian theology has been severely criticized in the past generation. On the one hand, its separation between speculative and evaluative judgments is highly questionable. Could these theologians justify their belief in the reality of the God supposedly encountered in Christ? On the other hand, does modern critical research support their conviction that scientific historiography can isolate the pure and original kernel of the gospel? Many would feel that both these questions must be negatively answered, leaving the Ritschlians imprisoned in vapid subjectivity.

28. *What Is Christianity?* (New York, paperback, 1957) 40.
29. *Ibid.*, 146.

4. SABATIER

Auguste Sabatier (1839–1901), as dean of the Faculty of Protestant Theology at Paris, popularized in France a religious Liberalism that combined something of Schleiermacher's sentimentalism with the moralism of Ritschl. In his *Outlines of a Philosophy of Religion* (French, 1896; ET 1897), he defines religion as "a conscious and willed relation into which the soul in distress enters with the mysterious power on which it feels that it and its destiny depend."[30] Prayer, he says, is religion in act—that is to say, real religion. Revelation is God's response to prayer, but since no prayer is in vain, revelation is always present, at least in germ, in prayer itself. Revelation is identical with the religious conscience; it is found in all religions, albeit in a more vital form in the Israelite prophets and in Jesus. Christianity is the definitive religion of humanity.[31] It consists initially in the revelatory experience that took place in the soul of Jesus, whereby he felt himself to be a son of God and a brother of all mankind. This experience, perfectly realized in Jesus, is to a lesser degree verified in all his disciples.[32]

Regarding the properties of revelation, Sabatier proclaims that it must necessarily be interior, evident, and progressive. "It will be interior, because God, not having phenomenal existence, can only reveal Himself to Spirit, and in the piety that He Himself inspires. . . . This inward revelation will also be evident. The contrary would imply a contradiction. He who says revelation says the veil withdrawn, the light come. . . . Lastly, this revelation will be progressive. It will be developed with the progress of the moral and religious life which God begets and nourishes in the bosom of humanity."[33]

Addressing himself next to the criterion of revelation, Sabatier stresses its immediacy. "Every divine revelation, every religious

30. *Outlines* (London, 1897) 27.
31. *Ibid.*, 138.
32. *Ibid.*, 139.
33. *Ibid.*, 54–57.

81

experience fit to nourish and sustain your soul, must be able to repeat and continue itself as an actual revelation and an individual experience in your own consciousness. . . . Thus the divine revelation which is not realised in us, and does not become immediate, does not exist for us."[34]

In his famous posthumous work, *The Religions of Authority and the Religion of the Spirit* (French, 1904; ET 1910), Sabatier attempted to ground in New Testament criticism his notion of a purely interior and spiritual Christianity without dogmas, rites, or hierarchy.

Sabatier's doctrine of revelation was at almost every point diametrically opposed to that of the Catholic Church in his day, as articulated, for example, by Vatican Council I. For a Catholic reply, by now considerably dated, one may consult Cuthbert Butler, O.S.B., *Religions of Authority* (London, 1930).

By the turn of the century Liberal Protestantism had already passed its zenith, partly as a result of the progress of scientific biblical criticism. Among the most influential studies was a small volume by Ritschl's pupil, Johannes Weiss, *Die Predigt vom Reiche Gottes* (1892), which established on exegetical grounds that Jesus' conception of the Kingdom of God was futuristic and visible, and that it in no way resembled the interior and purely ethical community envisaged by the Ritschlians. Once the radical discrepancy between the preaching of Jesus and the belief of modern Liberal Christians had been thus exposed, the way was open for works such as Albert Schweitzer's celebrated *Quest of the Historical Jesus* (German [1]1906), which has been called the "funeral oration" of the Liberal quest. By dramatizing Jesus as a fanatical futurist, Weiss, Schweitzer, and others focussed new interest on the eschatological element in the primitive Christian concept of revelation. While theological Liberalism survived well into the twentieth century, it was already clear by 1900 that the future of creative theology lay in some other direction, more consonant with the original thrust of the gospel.

34. *Ibid.*, 62–63.

E. Modernism

Although it flowered in the first decade of the twentieth century, Modernism belongs to the present chapter because it was in substance a Catholic echo of Protestant theology of the late nineteenth century. It was deeply influenced by the agnosticism of the neo-Kantians, the evolutionary pantheism of the neo-Hegelians, and the vitalism of the Pragmatists. In their theology of revelation the Modernists were especially indebted to Schleiermacher and Sabatier. They were labelled Modernists because they wanted to adapt Catholicism to what was valid in modern thought, even at the price of a certain discontinuity with the Church's own past teaching and institutional forms.

1. LOISY

Insofar as the movement had a founder or head, this position would have to be assigned to Alfred Loisy (1857–1940), a priest who taught Scripture at the Institut Catholique in Paris from 1884 to 1893, when his advanced views on biblical questions cost him his professorship. He continued to write prolifically, and in 1902 launched the Modernist movement with a short book, *The Gospel and the Church* (ET 1903). Ostensibly a Catholic answer to Harnack's *Wesen des Christentums,* this book makes the point that Christianity has no fixed essence since it is in continuing evolution. Its truth, like all human truth, is relative and progressive.

After this work was condemned by ecclesiastical authorities, Loisy followed it up with an apologia, *Autour d'un petit livre* (1903), in which he clearly sets forth the difference between his own concept of revelation and that received in the Catholic Church. After protesting against the "naive anthropomorphism" of his adversaries, he goes on to say:

What is called revelation can only be man's acquired consciousness of his relationship to God. What is the Christian revelation in its

83

principle and point of departure, except the perception in the soul of Christ of the relationship by which he himself was united to God and of that which binds all men to their heavenly Father? . . .

In contradistinction to perceptions of the rational and scientific order, the perception of religious truths is not the fruit of reason alone; it is a work of the intellect elicited, so to speak, under the pressure of the heart, of the religious and moral sentiment, and of the real will to good.[35]

On the basis of this experiential approach, Loisy questioned the very notion of revealed doctrines. "The truths of revelation live in the proclamations of faith before they are analyzed in doctrinal speculations. Their native form is a supernatural intuition and a religious experience, not an abstract consideration or a systematic definition of their object."[36] Dogmas for Loisy were a kind of scientific commentary on faith, enunciated by the Church in its efforts to mediate between faith itself and the scientific thinking of a given era. Dogmas were necessarily relative to the stage of intellectual and cultural development of those for and by whom they were formulated.

Loisy's conception of revelation has been well summarized by Latourelle: "To sum up, for Loisy, revelation is not a doctrine offered to our faith, an unchanging deposit of truths, but rather an intuitive and experimental perception, always in development (always becoming), of our relationship with God. Revelation, like dogma and theology, always evolves; it is always happening."[37]

2. TYRRELL

A youthful convert to Catholicism, George Tyrrell (1861–1909) entered the Society of Jesus in 1880. After teaching ethics for two years at Stonyhurst he became a regular contributor to *The Month*. His articles attracted the attention of

35. Paris, [2]1903, 195–97.
36. *Ibid.*, 200.
37. R. Latourelle, *Theology of Revelation*, 276.

Baron Friedrich von Hügel (1852–1925), who regarded him as a second Newman and introduced him to the work of Blondel and Loisy. Avidly taking up these new ideas, Tyrrell soon ran into doctrinal and disciplinary difficulties with his order. He was dismissed in 1906 for his adherence to Modernism. He died outside the Church, or at least without public reconciliation.

Tyrrell's idea of revelation is most clearly set forth in *Through Scylla and Charybdis* (1907), a book which aims to trace a middle course between rigid dogmatism and spineless pragmatism. Revelation as he conceived it consists in a quasi-mystical experience and is not to be identified with the intellectual component of that experience. The apostles received the fullness of revelation through their communion with Christ, and in their inspired writings gave classical expression to the Spirit of Christ. Our own assimilation of revelation must be a reenactment of the original prophetic experience, evoked through contact with the Church. Revelation cannot be communicated, but at most can be occasioned, by preaching and writing. The dogmas of the Church are not themselves revelation, but a merely human reaction to it. They serve to protect it, but are not endowed with scientific or philosophical infallibility. The dogmatic teaching of the Church, like the Church itself, is but a creature "to be used where it helps, to be left where it hinders." Tyrrell's many sound insights are vitiated by his excessive distrust of the conceptual element in revelation and by his predominantly pragmatic attitude toward the Church's teaching authority.[38]

3. THE OUTCOME OF THE MOVEMENT

The Modernist movement in France became associated with a pragmatic doctrine of truth, developed with a high degree of skill by Lucien Laberthonnière (1860–1932) and Edouard Le Roy (1870–1954). Le Roy, a disciple of Bergson, maintained that reality is a continuous flowing process to be grasped

38. On Tyrrell see further F. M. O'Connor, "Tyrrell: The Nature of Revelation," *Continuum* 3 (1965) 168–77; also *idem,* "George Tyrrell and Dogma," *Downside Review* 84 (1966) 16–34, 160–82.

intuitively in the life of action. Dogmatic formulations, in his view, are symbols of the aspirations of the moral life.

While many of the great figures asociated with Modernism remained loyally attached to the Church, several, like Loisy and Tyrrell, were excommunicated. Among these was the Italian disciple of Blondel, Ernesto Buonaiuti (1881–1946), who developed his master's philosophy of action in the direction of total immanentism.

In opposition to the Modernists, the Roman magisterium reaffirmed with renewed emphasis the teaching of Vatican I regarding the transcendent origin and permanent intellectual validity of revealed truth. In the decree *Lamentabili* (July 3, 1907) the Holy Office condemned 65 propositions, seven of which (nos. 20–26, *DS* 3420–26) have to do with revelation and dogma. Specially reprobated are the teachings that revelation is nothing but man's acquired consciousness of his relationship to God; that revelation was not complete with the apostles; that dogmas could, while religiously true, be historically false or doubtful; and that dogmas could be embraced by a practical judgment without being accepted as norms of belief.

Pius X, on September 8, 1907, issued the encyclical *Pascendi* (*DS* 3475–3500), which sets forth a full systematic version of the Modernist program, and concludes with the judgment, "If we take in the whole system at one glance, no one will be surprised when we define it as the synthesis of all heresies."[39] This presentation, based on ideas culled from various writers, does not perfectly correspond to the views of any particular individual. Some of the authors whose works were used as sources protested with some show of justice that they had not been condemned because their views had been caricatured.

The Oath Against Modernism[40] singles out and again condemns some of the leading Modernist errors. It denies that revelation is the product of "a blind religious sense issuing from the depths of the subconscious" and affirms that it is on the con-

39. This sentence, not included in *DS,* may be found in Denzinger-Bannwart ([30]1955) n. 2105.
40. *Sacrorum Antistites* (September 1, 1910); *DS* 3537–50.

86

trary the object of a truly religious assent. Revealed truth is held to come "from outside" and to be worthy of firm acceptance on the authority of God as witness. It is, moreover, certified by firm external arguments, especially miracles and prophecies, which are "very well suited to the mentality of men of all ages, including the present time" (*DS* 3539). Revelation, we are told, is not a creation of the human consciousness, nor is it gradually produced by human efforts, nor does it evolve by an indefinite progress. Rather, it is a doctrine received from the apostles and transmitted to us "*eodem sensu eademque semper sententia*" (*DS* 3541).

At a distance of sixty years the anti-Modernist documents appear definitely dated. While they settled the Modernist crisis on the practical level with strong disciplinary measures, they failed to provide a theoretical answer to the exegetical, historical, and philosophical difficulties with which the Modernists were grappling. Approaching these questions anew in a more serene atmosphere of discussion, one might find it possible to make more concessions to the Modernists and at the same time to safeguard, as they did not, the fundamentals of the Catholic notion of revelation.

F. Blondel

The most constructive Catholic response to the Modernist movement was that of a philosopher deeply concerned with combating the infidelity of his fellow intellectuals. Maurice Blondel (1861–1949), in his doctoral thesis for the École Normale in Paris (*L'Action*, 1893), dealt with the problem of man's need for the transcendent. The inner dialectic of human action, he maintained, reveals an ineluctable dynamism toward a goal which lies beyond man's power to achieve, but which, if it were to be offered as a supernatural gift, would be a genuine fulfilment.

Seeking a *via media* between a Modernist immanentism and an ultramontane extrinsicism, Blondel developed what he called the "method of immanence." In answer to Le Roy, he wrote on one occasion:

In order to avoid the narrow doctrine which sees in the supernatural only a servile heteronomy and which imposes God's gift after the fashion of a yoke—as though it were a matter of painfully grafting onto our body a new eye or a third arm—it is not necessary to fall into the contrary error, and to seek, in the name of a "principle of immanence" to reduce the supernatural to the role of a supreme expansion of our being—as though the apparent heteronomy ought to be resolved by a total human autonomy. . . . The role of the *method* of immanence is precisely to guard us against both extremes: it is to place us face to face with ourselves and with God; it is to make us measure the infinite disproportion between our nature and our destiny; it is to manifest, in its full rigor, the necessary and salutary heteronomy. . . .[41]

Not being a theologian by profession, Blondel was more concerned with the philosophical approaches to revelation than with the nature of revelation itself. But his principle of immanence clearly presupposes that revelatory knowledge must be partly produced by, as well as received into, the human mind. In his *Letter on Apologetics* (1896) he affirmed: "If among current ideas there is one which it regards as marking a definite advance, it is the idea, which is at bottom perfectly true, that nothing can enter into a man's mind which does not come out of him and correspond in some way to a need for development. . . ."[42]

In his *History and Dogma* (1904) Blondel set forth a theory of tradition corresponding to his dynamic view of revelation. Tradition, he taught, is not a matter of passively subscribing to a static, verbal deposit of faith, but of creatively articulating for one's own time the contents of the Church's lived experience of the realities of salvation. In such a view, doctrine becomes subordinate to a vital knowledge through connaturality. In the

41. B. de Sailly (=Blondel), "La Notion et le Rôle du Miracle," *Annales de philosophie chrétienne* (July 1907) 346f.
42. *Letter on Apologetics* (New York, 1964) 152.

whole Church, wrote Blondel, as in the individual believer, the normal movement is "from faith to dogma rather than from dogma to faith."[43]

Toward the end of his life Blondel returned to his original question regarding the relationship between the searchings of philosophy and the mysteries of Christian faith. He repeated in substance what he had already affirmed in *L'Action*—namely that "that which appears incredible, and which would seem to be impossible—that which men, all too humanly, have called 'folly and scandal'—Revelation presents to us as reality itself, as the absolute goal of the divine plan of creation." Surpassing all expectations the divine Word has personally assumed our nature in order to bring us into union with God. "This is the enigmatic message, the secret which no investigation could discover by the unaided forces of rational nature, but the truth which, once revealed, opens up an immense field of new problems and a whole series of solutions interconnected in the supple coherence of God's providential plan."[44]

During most of his career Blondel lived under a cloud, resented by the Modernists as a traitor to their movement, ignored by the free-thinking intellectuals, and suspected by the ultramontane conservatives of being a secret Modernist. Only in his declining years did he have the satisfaction of witnessing the beginning of a renewal in the Catholic theology of revelation, thanks to Joeph Maréchal, Teilhard de Chardin, Henri Bouillard, and many others who freely confessed their indebtedness to him. And, as Gregory Baum has remarked, the "Blondelian perspective that God is graciously present in the dynamics of human life and history" is one of the major themes in several documents of Vatican II, especially in the *Pastoral Constitution on the Church in the Modern World*.[45]

43. *History and Dogma, ibid.*, 279.
44. *La philosophie et l'esprit chrétien* 1 (Paris, 41950) 50.
45. Gregory Baum, *The Credibility of the Church Today* (New York, 1968) 13–15.

4. TWENTIETH-CENTURY PROTESTANTISM AND ANGLICANISM

The first two-thirds of the present century have seen lively developments in the theology of revelation. In general, theology has been torn between a dogmatic concern, prompting it to remain within the doctrinal traditions of the various churches, and an apologetical concern, inviting it to establish a maximum of common ground with the profane sciences. The theology of revelation has unquestionably undergone important changes in its unceasing dialogue—now polemical and now irenic—with disciplines such as history, philosophy, psychology, and sociology. At times theology has given the appearance of striving to find in revelation an independent sphere of competence, where the churchman could assert his authority in a decisive way in opposition to the inroads of modern secular thought.

A. History and Phenomenology of Religions

In the first two decades of the century a number of Protestant theologians became convinced that Christianity had arisen not through a special intervention from on high but through a syncretistic union of religions and philosophies already in existence—Jewish, Oriental, and Hellenistic. This point of view was learnedly defended by several professors at Göttingen University, including Mark Lidzbarski (a Polish Jew), Richard

Reitzenstein, and Wilhelm Bousset. These new theories of Christian origins acutely posed the problem of the relationship between revelation and history. If Christianity could be scientifically studied as one of the world's religions, was it still possible to regard it as God's definitive self-revelation?

1. TROELTSCH

Ernst Troeltsch (1865–1923) may be called the philosopher of the *Religionsgeschichtliche Schule*. After studying and lecturing at Göttingen, among other universities, he became professor at Heidelberg, where he remained for 21 years. Much influenced by Ritschl, he was troubled by the question whether Christianity, considered as a particular phase of man's religious history, could be accorded universal and absolute value. While acknowledging in the biblical portrait of Jesus an overpowering instance of God's revelatory presence, Troeltsch felt that the relativity of historical knowledge prevents us from maintaining that any given manifestation of the divine is unconditional and final. The formula "God in Christ" was acceptable to him only in the sense that "we revere in him the highest revelation of God accessible to us and make the picture of Jesus the focal point of all the self-manifestations of the godhead in our lives."[1]

The comparative study of religions persuaded Troeltsch that all vital religions rested on supernatural revelation in the sense of an ineffable, extraordinary experience associated with some powerful religious personality. He therefore adopted a "polymorphic" doctrine of religious truth, according to which God is apprehended in qualitatively diverse and irreducible forms by men of different races and cultures. Of Christianity he says:

Christianity could not be a religion of such a highly developed religious group if it did not possess a mighty spiritual power and truth; in short if it were not, in some degree, a manifestation of

1. *Die Bedeutung der Geschichtlichkeit Jesu für den Glauben* (Tübingen, 1911) 50.

the Divine Life itself. The evidence we have for this remains essentially the same, whatever may be our theory concerning absolute validity—it is the evidence of a profound inner experience. This experience is undoubtedly the criterion of its validity, but, be it noted, only of its validity *for us*. It is God's countenance as revealed to us; it is the way in which, being what we are, we receive, and react to, the revelation of God. It is binding upon us, and it brings us deliverance. It is final and unconditional for us, because we have nothing else, and because in what we have we can recognize the accents of divine love.

But this does not preclude the possibility that other racial groups living under entirely different cultural conditions, may experience in quite a different way, and may themselves also possess a religion which has grown up with them, and from which they cannot sever themselves so long at they remain what they are.[2]

Since Troeltsch's time, this type of religious pluralism has appealed to many learned students of human culture—for example, to Carl Jung, Simone Weil, and Arnold Toynbee.

2. OTTO

Like Troeltsch, Rudolf Otto (1869–1937) was a German Lutheran interested in the philosophy of religion and comparative religion. His religious philosophy owed much to Kant, Schleiermacher, and more immediately to J. K. Fries (1773–1843), who had sought a path to the divine through man's inner longings and sentiments rather than through rational argument and doctrinal revelation. As a philosopher Otto held that, to avoid absurdity in our thinking, we must postulate an Unconditioned Absolute, but speculative reason grasps this as "wholly other" and can speak of it only in negative terms. Religious experience, however, can supply a positive feeling of the reality and presence of this Absolute. Somewhat in the

2. "The Place of Christianity Among the World Religions," part I of *Christian Thought: Its History and Application* (New York, 1957), 55–56.

style of Schleiermacher, Otto engages in a close analysis of the phenomenology of religious feeling. In his famous study, *The Idea of the Holy* (German, [1]1917; ET 1923),[3] he gives a classic analysis of the "numinous," as he calls the specific quality of the religious object as such. Numinous experience, he concludes, involves a paradoxical fusion of terror and allurement (*"mysterium tremendum et fascinans"*). When combined with the ethically good (thanks to a "schematization" which occurs in the higher religions), the numinous coincides with the holy.

For Otto all human religions are based on grace or revelation (at least *revelatio generalis*). But this consideration does not lead him to abandon the pursuit of Christian theology for that of the philosophy of religion, as tended to be the case with Troeltsch. Finding in Christianity the supreme and unsurpassable manifestation of the holy, Otto chose to evaluate all other religious experience from the vantage point of Christian faith. "For the theologian the standpoint of the history of religions falls away like a dry leaf as soon as it has done its preparatory work."[4] Like the Modernists, Otto was distrustful of dogmatic formulas, esteeming them only for their evocative symbolic value. His phenomenological approach to the various religions has left a profound impress on later historians of religion, such as Gerardus van der Leeuw (1890–1950) and Mircea Eliade (1907–   ), as well as upon theologians such as Paul Tillich and John Macquarrie, both of whose ideas will be considered below.

3. SÖDERBLOM

The Swedish Lutheran archbishop of Uppsala, Nathan Söderblom (1866–1931), as a young pastor spent seven years in Paris as a student of the history of religions (1894–1901). He then taught theology at Uppsala and Leipzig before being named archbishop in 1913. After World War I he devoted

3. Frequently reprinted.
4. *The Kingdom of God and the Son of Man* (rev., 1951) 375.

his talents primarily to the fledgling ecumenical movement, and in 1925 organized the great international conference on Life and Work held at Stockholm.

Influenced by Schleiermacher, Ritschl, and von Hügel, Söderblom attempted to do justice to religious intuition, history and mysticism in his theology of revelation. While discerning revelation in some wide sense at the source of all religions, he maintained that revelation in the strict sense is found only in individuals in whom the consciousness of the infinite and the longing for the ideal expressed themselves with such clarity that they became a beacon light for other men in quest of salvation. These two passions reached their highest fulfilment in Christ; but Christ himself, according to Söderblom, stands at the origin of a long series of personalities in whom his revelatory function has been continued. In modern times, Söderblom believed, the light of the gospel should be shown forth by a deep concern for peace and social justice. In his dedication to secular ecumenism he believed that he was giving new power and relevance to the Christian revelation.[5]

Söderblom bequeathed to the Swedish theologians of the twentieth century (including Aulén, Nygren, Tor Andrae, Lindblom, and others) an intense interest in the psychology of religious experience and in comparative religion. His ideas on revelation are chiefly to be found in his early work, *The Nature of Revelation* (1903, reissued by the author in 1930) and in his 1931 Gifford lectures, *The Living God*.

B. Dialectical Theology

1. BARTH

Son of a Swiss pastor, Karl Barth (1886–   ) made his theological studies at Berlin under Harnack and at Marburg

5. In this connection see C. J. Curtis, *Söderblom: Ecumenical Pioneer* (Minneapolis, 1967), which studies Söderblom's processive theology of revelation with a view to its contemporary relevance.

under W. Herrmann. He accepted all the premises of neo-Kantian Liberalism. Kant and Schleiermacher were his favorite authors. In 1909 he became a Calvinist pastor in Switzerland and soon afterward found his way into the Christian socialist movement. The exigencies of preaching and the shaking experiences of World War I convinced him of the inadequacies of Liberal theology. Reading Paul and Luther with fresh eyes, he published in 1919 his celebrated commentary on Romans. Re-edited in 1922, it became the *magna charta* of a theological revolution in continental Protestantism.[6]

Since Kant, Protestant theologians had generally sought to erect religion on the foundation of man's immanent tendencies. Troeltsch appealed to the "religious *a priori*" and Otto to the innate category of the numinous. In any such system Christianity can appear as a fulfilment, possibly the highest fulfilment, of human aspirations; but revelation is necessarily confined within the natural order and limited according to man's antecedent capacity for religious experience.

Central to the Barthian view, especially as expressed in the *Römerbrief*, is the contrast between religion and revelation. The former is the outreach of sinful, fallen man toward God. The latter is the act whereby the utterly transcendent and unattainable God graciously comes to man. Christianity is seen as revelation—that is, as a downward movement from God. God's word falls perpendicularly "like a stone" into the human situation. What Christ came to bring is not a new form of piety or religious experience, but a revelation of God, the totally other. Man's reaction to revelation, whether in the privacy of his individual experience or in the community of his collective history, is always vitiated by sin. Thus religion, even in a Christian context, is to some extent a perversion of revelation.

Dealing as it did with God's judgment on mankind, Barth's early work was aptly called "crisis theology." This divine judgment (*krisis*) is conceived in terms of the Hegelian dialectic of

6. ET from [6]ed. by E. C. Hoskyns, *Epistle to the Romans* (London, 1933).

negation and sublation. Thus revelation is seen as crushing human pride and thereby raising man from sin. It paradoxically manifests both God's wrath and his grace in indivisible unity. Precisely in his chastisement God shows his mercy. Because of this *complexio oppositorum* Barth's theology has also been called dialectical.

The paradoxical judgment of God, according to Barth, comes to us in Christ. He is in the concrete God's revelation to man, "the eternal as event." In him the timeless intersects with time (and their meeting, in Barth's early theologizing, is regarded as merely tangential). As crucified, Jesus becomes the risen one; the message of the Cross is that of eternal life. In saying "no" to all human possibilities, God effects a new creation in Christ.

Barth attacks both the old rationalism and the new historicism. Rationalism, he finds, neglects the event-character of revelation, reducing it to a series of timeless truths. Historicism on the other hand would overlook the divine dimensions of the event, absorbing revelation into the continuum of profane history, and thus undermining the absolute character of Christianity (see Troeltsch). In his insistence on the "infinite qualitative distance" between the temporal and the eternal, Barth harks back to Kierkegaard.

After his dialectical period, Barth began to develop a theology which takes as its central concept the "word of God." God's word, Barth maintains, comes in three forms—as revealed word, as written word, and as preached word. The revealed word is Christ, the incarnate Logos, who alone is revelation in an unqualified sense. The written word of the Bible and the preached word of the Church are revelation and word of God insofar as God may be pleased to encounter us through these means. The word of God is therefore the event by which God comes to us in Christ. Barth's doctrine of the word of God is very fully developed in first two half-volumes of his monumental *Church Dogmatics* (1932ff.; ET 1936ff.).[7]

7. Barth summarized his views on revelation in his contribution to J. Baillie and H. Martin, *Revelation* (London, 1937). Among the many

Barth's theological outlook has mellowed over the years. In his early work he insisted chiefly on the inadequacy of man's natural powers to attain the divine (*"finitum non capax infiniti"*), but in recent years he prefers to stress the gracious condescension by which God has bridged the chasm and communicated with his creatures. If there is no *analogia entis* serving as the basis for a natural theology, there is nevertheless, as Barth points out in his later writings, an *analogia gratiae* which enables the believer to speak correctly of God. Barth places great confidence in the value of the Church's confessions of faith as representing the way in which believing Christians must speak about God. Many of Barth's Protestant colleagues are ill at ease with his confessional dogmatism; they accuse him of intolerance, exclusiveness, and "transcendental irresponsibility." This charge of irresponsibility finds some echo in Catholic critics, who generally complain that Barth unduly separates the realms of faith and natural knowledge.

2. BRUNNER

Educated like Barth in Liberal theology, H. Emil Brunner (1889–1966), too, served as a Reformed pastor in Switzerland before becoming a theology professor. Like Barth, also, he rebelled against the psychologism of Schleiermacher and the historicism of Troeltsch, and came to the conviction that God's revelatory word immeasurably surpasses all the immanent possibilities of human development. In seeking categories with which to speak of revelation, Brunner drew heavily upon the personalist philosophies of Ferdinand Ebner and Martin Buber.

An important point of difference between Barth and Brunner may be found in their respective attitudes toward philosophical anthropology and the philosophy of religion. Barth repudiates these disciplines; Brunner regards them as necessary. There

---

studies on Barth's doctrine of revelation one may mention as especially useful for our present purposes, H. Bouillard, *Karl Barth* (3 vols. in 2, Paris, 1957).

must be a point of contact, he insists, between revelation and reason, a common ground of discussion for believers and unbelievers. Christianity must study man in his actual condition and find in the human situation a "point of insertion" for the gospel (whence arose the celebrated Barth-Brunner controversy concerning the *"Anknüpfungspumkt"*). Brunner even admits a natural theology in the sense that the human mind, despite original sin, does not cease to be fundamentally *capax Dei*.

Brunner's concept of revelation attempts to rectify what he considered to be two major distortions. The first of these is that of Protestant Liberal theology, which compromised the uniqueness and transcendence of God's revealing word; the other is the petrifaction of revelation in both Protestant and Catholic "orthodoxy," which depicted revelation as a desposit of propositional truths. The specific quality of the biblical revelation, according to Brunner, is that God comes to us as "absolute subject." As such he cannot be comprehended by conceptual, objectifying knowledge. He encounters us interpersonally through an event that inwardly transforms us. Revelation achieves itself in the inner change by which the recipient makes the absolute surrender of faith. Faith differs from every other form of knowledge since, instead of giving us mastery of an object, it places us at the disposal of the Absolute Subject.

Viewing revelation exclusively as a personal encounter, Brunner was led to deny that its contents can be legitimately expressed in propositional form. Doctrine for him, as for the Modernists, was merely a human reaction to revelation, always fallible and approximative. Dogma is a Hellenization of the gospel; it substitutes speculative knowledge for proclamation. The Church for Brunner is an interpersonal community. It is not, or should not be, an institution.

Discounting his polemical negations, Brunner's positive account of revelation has much to commend it.[8] The following

8. See the balanced appraisal of Joseph J. Smith, *Emil Brunner's Theology of Revelation* (Manila, 1967); also P. K. Jewett, *Emil Brunner's Concept of Revelation* (London, 1954), and H. E. Hatt, *Encountering Truth* (Nashville, 1966).

definition of revelation comes close to the personalistic views of many contemporary Catholic theologians:

In all religions "revelation" means a process through which something that had previously been hidden from man is disclosed, a mystery is mysteriously manifested, a knowledge that comes from outside the normal sphere of knowledge, which cannot be achieved by man, but must be given to him, enters suddenly and unexpected into his life, and not only increases his knowledge, but has significance for his life, for good or ill. These characteristics are also represented in the Biblical idea of revelation, but they are provided with a double signature, which gives them a completely new meaning. This double signature is absoluteness and personal character. For this very reason, however, as we shall see, an abstract definition of revelation is impossible; its meaning can be grasped only through the historically "given."[9]

Barth and Brunner, especially the former, restored to modern Protestant theology a sense of the divine transcendence and of the total commitment demanded by faith. They shifted the accent back from religion, where Liberal Protestantism had placed it, to revelation. Pius XII, in the Encyclical *Humani generis*, expressed both gratification and dissatisfaction with this trend. After listing various errors to be found in non-Catholic theology, he added:

Amid all this welter of speculations, we find some comfort in the contemplation of a different school of thinkers. Not a few of the moderns, reacting from the dogmas of the rationalism in which they were brought up, are thirsting afresh for the wells of divine revelation. They recognize and proclaim the Word of God, preserved for us in Holy Scriptures, as the foundation of Christian teaching. But many of them, alas, in their determination to hold fast by God's Word, banish the exercise of human reason. The more loudly they extol the authority of God revealing, the more bitter is their con-

9. E. Brunner, *Revelation and Reason* (London, 1947) 22–23. Brunner further evolves his doctrine of revelation in *Truth as Encounter* (Philadelphia, 1964) and *The Word of God and Modern Man* (Richmond, Va., 1964).

tempt for the teaching office of the Church, although our Lord Jesus Christ himself instituted it as the means by which the truths God has revealed should be safeguarded and interpreted.[10]

3. BULTMANN

Rudolf Bultmann (1884–) was, like Barth, a pupil of Gunkel and Herrmann, but he specialized more in exegesis and served as Professor of New Testament at Marburg from 1921 to 1955. In his epoch-making *History of the Synoptic Tradition* ([1]1921) he established himself as the leader of the Form Critical school.

Bultmann began his theological career in close association with Barth and Friedrich Gogarten (1887–1967). He complained, as did they, that Liberal theology had failed to acknowledge the total otherness of the God who encounters us in revelation. Liberalism, said Bultmann, erroneously treated revelation not as an "eschatological" event, summoning us to the decision of faith, but as an occurrence within history. "Thus man and humanity simply as such are taken to be creative; and what one can perceive in moral achievements and the phenomena of culture has the value of revelation."[11] Catholic and Protestant Orthodoxy, according to Bultmann, made the error of attempting to fit revelation into the generic category of knowledge, thus setting it over against rational knowledge as a competitor. In opposition to both these alleged errors, Bultmann reverts to the idea of revelation he finds in the New Testament, especially in Paul and John, according to which the subject and object of revelation are nothing less than the living God himself insofar as he summons us to authentic existence. As Bultmann puts it (p. 85) in the essay just cited:

What, then, has been revealed? Nothing at all, so far as the question concerning revelation asks for doctrines—doctrines, say, that no

10. Para. 8, Knox transl.; cf. *DB 2307,* not in *DS.*
11. "Revelation in the New Testament," *Existence and Faith* (New York, 1960) 69.

man could have discovered for himself—or for mysteries that become known once and for all as soon as they are communicated. On the other hand, however, everything has been revealed, insofar as man's eyes are opened concerning his own existence and he is once again able to understand himself. It is as Luther says: "Thus, in going out of himself, God brings it about that we go into ourselves; and through knowledge of him he brings us knowledge of ourselves."

The most famous of Bultmann's essays is a ringing appeal for the demythologizing of the Christian message. Entitled "New Testament and Mythology," this essay first appeared in 1941.[12] Revelation, Bultmann here maintains, cannot consist in historical facts, abstract doctrines, or timeless myths. It is the divine action whereby God meets man in the preaching of the word. The Christian kerygma—God's message of redemption in Jesus Christ—is the effective instrument by which men are called to salvation. Making use of Martin Heidegger's existential categories, Bultmann explains that when man, opening himself to the demands of love, accepts in total obedience the message of God's saving action, he escapes the anxiety of his normal worldly condition and achieves newness of life.

Bultmann's critics have found several major difficulties in his doctrine of revelation.[13] Barth and his followers complain that in Bultmann, no less than in Schleiermacher, revelation is anthropocentrically viewed in terms of man's inner needs, to which it is exactly tailored. Bultmann's more traditional fellow Lutherans protest that he falls into a new gnosticism, substituting salvation by a *message* about Christ for salvation by Christ himself, as a person of flesh and blood. Would the report about Jesus, they ask, have any saving value unless Jesus, as a person, stood behind it? Theologians influenced by secular

12. Reprinted in H. W. Bartsch (ed.), *Kerygma and Myth* 1 (New York, 1961) 1–44.
13. Many criticisms are found in the series *Kerygma and Mythos*, 2 vols. of which are available in ET. See also J. Macquarrie, *An Existentialist Theology* (New York, paperback, 1965) and *The Scope of Demythologizing* (New York, paperback, 1966).

humanism, such as Paul van Buren[14] and Schubert Ogden,[15] object that Bultmann shows a dogmatic narrowness in making salvation depend unconditionally on man's hearing the Christian preaching. If salvation consists in the achievement of authentic existence, they argue, it should be a real human possibility even for those to whom the gospel has not been preached.

Some of the ambiguities in Bultmann's position have been skillfully brought out by Fritz Buri (1907–   ), professor of dogmatics at the University of Basel. In a critical essay on Bultmann,[16] Buri attacked what is for Bultmann the heart of the Christian revelation—the kerygma concerning the crucified and risen Jesus. On what basis, asked Buri, does Bultmann affirm God's special saving presence in the event of Christian proclamation? For Buri the kerygma is nothing but the last remnant of mythology.

In a theology of existence heavily influenced by Jaspers, Buri has insisted on the positive value and inevitability of mythological language. Without myth man simply cannot speak of personal responsibility in its unconditioned character (a datum of the moral consciousness as self-evident to Buri as it was to Kant). Buri adheres to the biblical Christ symbol, but he insists that the content of that symbol refers not merely to a special time of salvation but to something coextensive with the universal history of mankind.[17]

Karl Jaspers (1883–1969), who has himself engaged in long polemical exchanges with Bultmann, agrees with Buri that the

14. *The Secular Meaning of the Gospel* (New York, 1963; paperback, 1966).

15. *Christ Without Myth* (New York, 1961).

16. "Entmytholigisierung oder Entkerygmatisierung der Theologie," *Kerygma und Mythos* 2 (Hamburg, 1952) 85–101. Barth, commenting on this essay, finds in Buri's "ultraradicalization of Bultmann's radicalism" a kind of *reductio ad absurdum* of Bultmann's principles. See K. Barth, "Rudolf Bultmann—An Attempt to Understand Him," *Kerygma and Myth* 2 (London, 1962) 130.

17. In *How Can We Still Speak Responsibly of God?* (Philadelphia, 1968), Buri outlines his program for a "theology of responsibility" and proposes a new kind of Christian natural theology as the basis for an encounter among man's different religious heritages.

102

biblical redemptive history has great value as a mythical expression of truth to those who believe it. It helps them to grow in awareness of their situation before the transcendent; it directs their moral attitudes, hopes, and goals. Jaspers, however, accuses Bultmann of a narrow and intolerant orthodoxy in his defense of "the most alienating, the most outlandish of beliefs"—the Lutheran dogma of justification by faith alone.[18]

Under severe attack from both the right and the left, the Bultmannians have begun to find that it is necessary to qualify somewhat their master's doctrine of salvation through the Christian kerygma. We shall discuss some of the so-called post-Bultmannians (Fuchs, Ebeling) in a later section of this chapter.

C. American Theology

1. FUNDAMENTALISM

In the early years of the century the leading American theologians were biblically minded conservatives such as the Princeton Theological Seminary Professor, Benjamin B. Warfield (1851–1921), a staunch defender of Presbyterian orthodoxy according to the letter of the Westminster Confession. Warfield contended that the redemptive acts of God in history were mute except insofar as they were illuminated by the inspired word. The word of God for him meant the Bible. As he argued in 1909: the Scriptures alone, of all the revelations God may have given, are extant; thus they must be judged to be, as a whole and in all their parts, the one and only revelation of God accessible to man.[19]

The importation of Liberal German biblical scholarship, including the "higher criticism," together with new scientific developments in the fields of paleontology and human evolution,

18. Cf. K. Jaspers, "Myth and Religion," in K. Jaspers and R. Bultmann, *Myth and Christianity* (New York, 1958) 47–51. For a fuller statement of Jaspers' position see his *Philosophical Faith and Revelation* (London, 1967).

19. *Revelation and Inspiration* (New York, 1927) 33.

threatened what was for many American Protestants the mainstay of faith—the "obvious meaning" of the Bible. Inevitably, there was a strong defensive reaction, known as Fundamentalism. This movement is generally dated from the appearance in 1909–15 of twelve small volumes entitled, *The Fundamentals: A Testimony to the Truth.* These booklets, containing articles by various authors, including Warfield himself, defended the total inerrancy of the Bible and a number of biblically founded doctrines such as the divinity of Christ, his virgin birth, and his bodily resurrection. The spirit of Fundamentalism is aptly summarized in the statement of William Jennings Bryan, at the Scopes trial in 1925, that evolution stands condemned because the great majority of Christians understand the Bible as opposed to it. Fundamentalism was given some theological support by conservatives such as Warfield, the Scottish Presbyterian James Orr,[20] and the Princeton professor J. Gresham Machen (who in 1929 resigned to found his own conservative seminary in Philadelphia).

Since about 1930, conservative evangelical theology, in the United States and abroad, has been seeking to shed the Fundamentalist label and to identify itself with less reactionary positions. For the present mood of this movement one may consult the symposium, *Revelation and the Bible,* edited in 1958 by Carl F. H. Henry. The contributors, according to Henry's preface, "discuss biblical revelation with full reference to God's saving acts, and thereby contemplate revealed ideas in association with redemptive history. They do full justice to the historical and personal elements in special revelation."[21]

2. THE NIEBUHRS

The brothers Reinhold Niebuhr (1892–   ) and Helmut Richard Niebuhr (1894–1962), whose names are associated

20. *Revelation and Inspiration* (New York, 1910).
21. *Revelation and the Bible* (Grand Rapids, 1958) 9.

respectively with Union Theological Seminary in New York and with Yale Divinity School, are outstanding among American-born Protestants for their contributions to the theology of revelation. Both of them are heavily indebted to recent continental European thinkers. They in some measure fuse the historical relativism of Troeltsch, the dialectical thinking of Barth, and the personalism of Brunner. Both of them stress that God's revelation comes through *Heilsgeschichte,* and that the Christ-event, as the supremely luminous point of history, becomes for the Christian believer the supreme revelation of both God and man.

Reinhold Niebuhr in his magnum opus, *The Nature and Destiny of Man* (2 vols, 1941–43), maintains that the Atonement is the heart of the Christian revelation. In the Cross of Christ, viewed with the eyes of faith, are disclosed the justice and mercy of God, the immensity of human sin, and the destructive power of evil. The Cross makes it clear that redemption must come from beyond history, and thus enables us to look forward in hope. The symbol of the resurrection, according to Niebuhr, "is the final expression of the certainty about the power of God to complete our fragmentary life as well as the power of his love to purge it of the false completions in which all history is involved."[22] Like other biblical symbols, the resurrection must be taken seriously but not literally. It should not be used as a miraculous proof of faith. Faith, according to Niebuhr, cannot be demonstrated to those who stand outside it, but it can be seen from within to provide "a source and centre of an interpretation of life, more adequate than alternative interpretations, because it comprehends all of life's antinomies and contradictions into a system of meaning and is conducive to a renewal of life."[23]

H. Richard Niebuhr in his *The Meaning of Revelation* (1941) is concerned with finding an escape from the agnostic consequences of Troeltsch's historical relativism. His solution,

22. *Faith and History* (London, 1949) 169.
23. *Ibid.,* 187.

partly inspired by Barth, is that the theologian, operating within the perspectives of the Church's faith, may properly appeal not to technical ("external") history—which leads to doubt rather than to faith—but to confessional ("internal") history, that is, to the living memory of the community to which he belongs.

Revelation means for us that part of our inner history which illuminates the rest of it and which is itself intelligible. Sometimes when we read a difficult book, seeking to follow a complicated argument, we come across a luminous sentence from which we can go forward and backward and so attain some understanding of the whole. Revelation is like that. In his *Religion in the Making* Professor Whitehead has written such illuminating sentences and one of them is this: "Rational religion appeals to the direct intuition of special occasions, and to the elucidatory power of its concepts for all occasions." The special occasion to which we appeal in the Christian church is called Jesus Christ, in whom we see the righteousness of God, his power and wisdom. But from that special occasion we also derive the concepts which make possible the elucidation of all the events in our history. Revelation means this intelligible event which makes all other events intelligible.[24]

Like his elder brother, H. Richard Niebuhr insists on a purely symbolic understanding of the ancient dogmas of the Church and refuses to seek support for faith in miraculous occurrences.

The Niebuhrs' personalistic approach to salvation history takes due notice of the subjective dispositions required for the interpretation of faith; but their unwillingness to speak in ontological terms makes one wonder if they have really escaped the subjectivism of the Liberal theologians whom they severely criticize. As John Macquarrie remarks,[25] it must be possible to get beyond dramatic pictures in our analysis of what is involved in the personal encounter of God. If revelation is a reality, there must be a way of expressing it in terms of our understanding of being. This effort need not, and should not, lead back into a crude objectivism.

24. *The Meaning of Revelation* (New York, paperback, 1967) 68–69.
25. *Twentieth Century Religious Thought* (New York, 1963) 350.

3. TILLICH

Paul Tillich (1886–1965) was born in Brandenburg. After classical studies in Berlin, he obtained a doctorate in philosophy before studying theology at Halle under Martin Kähler and others. He wrote both his philosophical and his theological dissertations on Schelling. Having served as an army chaplain in World War I, he taught philosophy and theology at various German universities and was an active leader in the movement of Religious Socialism. Dismissed from his professorate at Frankfurt by the Nazis, he came to New York, where he taught at Union Theological Seminary from 1933–1955. Later he taught at Harvard Divinity School and Chicago Divinity School. His ideas on revelation are most fully presented in his *Systematic Theology*, vol. 1.[26]

Because he drew his ideas from many fonts, and operated on many frontiers, Tillich is hard to classify. He was indebted to the idealism of Schelling and Hegel, the Romanticism of Schleiermacher and Otto, the historicism of Troeltsch, the dialectical thinking of Barth, the existentialism of Kierkegaard, the ontology of Heidegger, and the depth psychology of Jung. He aimed to be both traditional and modern, faithfully Christian and yet meaningful to the secular mind. Perhaps the most philosophically minded of the great Protestant theologians of this century, he brilliantly integrated his ideas on revelation with his ontology.

Unlike Barth, Tillich took his starting point from man's existential situation—that of finiteness and anxiety—which gives rise to concern. Man's supreme concern, which is to find the ultimate ground of his being, gives rise to the question of God. But man cannot by his own free activity find the answer to that question, for his ordinary knowledge is limited by the subject-object dichotomy, which God transcends.

Revelation, then, is the leap whereby it is given to man to

26. Chicago, 1951.

encounter God as the ground of his being. As its objective correlative this extraordinary apprehension (ecstasy) demands an extraordinary event (miracle) which signalizes the presence of the divine. In summary, revelation may be called the self-manifestation of God through miracle and ecstasy.

Revelation may occur at any place or time, but the final and universal revelation, according to Tillich, is that which occurs in Jesus as the Christ. This revelation was made originally through Jesus to his immediate disciples. By preaching, writing, and liturgy, the Church produces numinous situations in which the revelation is handed on to others ("dependent revelation"). When the Christian revelation comes to men it heals their existential conflicts and estrangement; it gives them a share in the "new being" which is Christ.

Looking on myth and symbol as the language of ultimate concern, Tillich was critical of Bultmann's call to "demythologize" the gospel. He agreed with Bultmann, however, that the biblical myths must be "broken"—that is, understood in a non-literal sense. Like Bultmann, therefore, Tillich was quite radical in reinterpreting the ancient dogmas in ways that he considered appropriate for our culture. The *cardo salutis* in this theology appeared to be not Jesus as a person but rather "the biblical portrait of Jesus as the Christ." He regarded it as evident, however, that this portrait was not a free creation of the imagination of the primitive community, but a symbolically accurate representation of the actual Jesus in his revelatory function.

Although he did not come to the United States till the age of 46, Tillich became quite at home in his new country, where he published his most important works. He made a profound theological impression in New York, Cambridge, and Chicago, and his influence continues through former students and friends such as Langdon Gilkey, Carl Braaten, Jerald Brauer, and Thomas Altizer, each of whom has developed in his own direction.

108

4. HARVEY

Van A. Harvey, born in 1926 of missionary parents in China, received his B.D. and Ph.D. at Yale, where he imbibed the influence of H. Richard Niebuhr. After teaching at Princeton from 1954 to 1958, he moved to the Perkins School of Theology at Southern Methodist University, where he taught from 1958 to 1968, specializing in the problems of revelation and theological method. His *The Historian and the Believer*[27] propounds a theory of revelation through interpreted historical events which confessedly owes much to Rudolf Bultmann, H. R. Niebuhr, Alan Richardson, and Paul Tillich.

Every event, Harvey maintains, has a number of potential meanings. The more fundamental the meaning one finds in an event, the more capable that event becomes of being transformed into myth "where 'myth' does not mean a false story but a highly selective story that is used to convey the basic self-understanding of a person or a community" (p. 257).

By revelation Harvey understands a religious paradigmatic event; that is to say, an event that is believed to focus some insight into the nature of reality, insofar as this bears on the human quest for liberation and fulfilment. The Christian revelation is the interpretation of the total human situation in terms of a parable in which Jesus Christ constitutes the key image. The New Testament presents us with a variety of images of Jesus, portraying him as he appeared to the believing community. Christian faith involves the acceptance of the New Testament image of Jesus as one that illuminates our experience and our relationship to the object of our ultimate concern. While one cannot prove that the Christian image of Jesus is true, apologetics might be able to show that the Christian perspective has a viability, intelligibility, and comprehensiveness not found in the alternative perspectives.

Harvey's view of revelation responds to a widely felt need

27. New York, 1966. See especially ch. 8.

to avoid traditional theological jargon and to ground the Christian vision as fully as possible in history and experience. He avoids the extravagance of secular thinkers such as Paul van Buren, who have practically eliminated the concept of revelation. But still the question must be asked whether, in his efforts to meet the modern secular mind, Harvey has not unduly reduced the contents of the Christian affirmation. While giving an enlightening account of the Christian image of Jesus, he does not sufficiently explain what there was in Jesus himself to justify the transcendent role attributed to him by the Church. Harvey shies away from affirming anything about Jesus that might not win the assent of the non-believing historian.

D. British Theology

1. NEO-HEGELIANISM

Anglican theology in the nineteenth century was dominated by the great Cambridge exegetes, Joseph B. Lightfoot, Fenton J. A. Hort, and Brooke F. Westcott. Toward the end of the century there was a certain revival of speculative theology, especially within the movement known as "Liberal Catholicism," which sought to effect a synthesis between traditional theology and contemporary culture. The chief manifesto of this movement was the publication in 1889 of *Lux Mundi,* a series of studies by various authors on the religion of the Incarnation. Charles Gore and J. R. Illingworth in their contributions to this work attempted to show that the acceptance of the new critical standpoint in Scripture studies, and of new currents in idealistic philosophy, could be reconciled with full loyalty to the Catholic faith according to the ancient Creeds.

Some of the neo-Hegelians of this period, such as Edward Caird (1835–1908), strove to ground Christianity in an evolutionary idealism, in which Christ appeared as the incarnation of the universal idea of divinized humanity, the goal of the entire evolutionary process. Caird sought to combine the immanence of pantheism with the transcendence of theism. For him all reality was revelation, since everything manifests the divine. The dogmas of Christianity were in his view hypotheses to be confirmed by philosophy.

A different variety of neo-Hegelianism took shape in the absolute idealism of F. H. Bradley (1846–1924), who maintained that the Absolute alone is the real and that everything relative or mutable is mere appearance. Christianity, according to Bradley, is transcendent, "conscious of itself above time, and yet revealing itself in the historical growth of spiritual experience." In his view it made no real difference for Christian faith whether Jesus as a historical figure had actually lived and taught in Galilee and actually died in Jerusalem on a cross. The truth of Christianity, he maintained, was universal and eternal, and therefore independent of temporal occurrences.[28]

2. TEMPLE

Son of an Anglican archbishop, William Temple (1881–1944) studied at Balliol College, Oxford, where he absorbed the Hegelianism of Caird and Bosquanet. He became a priest in 1909, Archbishop of York in 1929, and Archbishop of Canterbury in 1942. As an active churchman, he, like Nathan Söderblom in Sweden, played a leading role in the social apostolate and the ecumenical movement. His theological writings are interesting for the way in which they seek to set forth an orthodox Christology and theology of revelation in Hegelian philosophical categories.

The whole of nature, in Temple's view, is a self-manifestation of the Divine Mind. "But the main field of Revelation must be in the history of men, rather than in the ample spaces of nature," for it is "in dealing with persons as persons that personality most truly expresses itself."[29] While the regular

28. *The Principles of Logic* 2 (Oxford, rev., [2]1922), Terminal Essay 8, 688–90; cf. J. Macquarrie, *An Existentialist Theology,* 190–91.
29. *Nature, Man, and God* (New York, 1953) 305.

routine of nature in some measure manifests God's will, "there may come occasions where action of a special and specially characteristic quality is required and the action so taken may be in an especial degree revealing; such acts are commonly called miracles."[30]

The mighty acts of God, therefore, are the primary vehicle of revelation. The biblical writers appeal to the events of the Exodus and especially to the life, death, and resurrection of Christ as the objective manifestation of God. Temple, indeed, goes so far as to assert that revelation consists neither in correct doctrine, nor in the words of the Bible, but in the events themselves.[31]

Yet Temple goes on to say that the events themselves are not revelation unless there is a prophetic mind present and capable of appreciating their significance. Revelation results from "the coincidence of event and appreciation," both of which are controlled by God. "He guides the process; He guides the minds of men; the interaction of the process and the minds which are alike guided by Him is the essence of revelation."[32]

Temple's effort to do justice to both the objective and the subjective aspects of revelation has been widely acclaimed, but many of his critics feel that he separates the two aspects excessively. For a balanced appraisal one fittingly may quote A. M. Ramsey, who was destined to succeed him, first as Archbishop of York and then as Archbishop of Canterbury:

Temple's teaching about Revelation has had immense influence. It was congruous with much in the trend of English theology since *Lux Mundi,* and of liberal theology generally since Ritschl: and while it treated the event as primary, and faith as a relation to a Person, it conserved the importance of dogma in a way that Ritschlianism never did. But it is as a theory vulnerable. The distinction between history as objective and interpretation as subjective breaks

30. Quoted without specified source by F. A. Iremonger, *William Temple* (London, 1948) 534.

31. W. Temple, contribution to J. Baillie and H. Martin (eds.), *Revelation* (London, 1937) 83–124; especially 103–107.

32. *Nature, Man, and God,* 312.

down, since it is hard to define history except as event *plus* inter-pretation. The distinction between the stage of event and the stage of proposition breaks down, since interpretative propositions enter into the very record of the events. Nor, if the dogmas are neces-sary to enable the revelation to be conserved by the Church and grasped by the faithful, can they be held to lie outside the act of revelation. These criticisms suggest that Temple's formulation of the nature of revelation considerably over-simplifies the issues with a measure of false antithesis.

None the less, Temple's thesis concerning revelation, vulnerable as it may be, has had a most salutary influence. It has helped in the recovery of the Biblical view that in revelation events come first, and that the idea of a corpus of revealed propositions standing on its own ground is intolerable. It has helped to keep central the con-viction that it is towards a Person that faith is directed, and that revelation is dominated by that fact. Temple's presentation brings to the centre what should be at the centre, and thus helps us on our way towards a comprehensive view of revelation in which event and interpretation, Person, proposition and inspired imagery have each its own place.[33]

In connection with Temple one may appropriately mention the Anglo-Catholic, Lionel S. Thornton, C.R. (1884–1960), who in his *Revelation and the Modern World*[34] outlined his "organic" theory of revelation. Thornton attempts to avoid the pitfalls of Liberalism and Fundamentalism by an elaborate series of correspondences in which the entire Christian mystery is viewed as an organic whole built about Christ as center of all creation. While repudiating all forms of evolutionary ideal-ism, and insisting on the divine transcendence, Thornton makes use of modern process philosophies to illuminate the cosmic headship of Christ, as set forth by Paul and Irenaeus. In re-vealing himself, God, according to Thornton, necessarily takes on the "form of the servant," but revelation succeeds in master-ing its environment because it is God who takes on this humble form.

33. A. M. Ramsey, *From Gore to Temple* (London, 1960) 152–53.
34. The first of his three volumes collectively entitled *The Form of the Servant* (Westminster, Eng., 1950).

3. DODD

Charles Harold Dodd (1884–   ), an English Congregationalist who has taught at Oxford and Cambridge, enjoys the
highest esteem as a New Testament exegete. While he has not
set forth a developed theology of revelation, his biblical studies
have led him to explore the relations between history and
revelation. His early views on revelation may be studied in *The
Authority of the Bible* ([1]1928; rev. 1960),[35] where he works
mostly with the categories of religious experience, and echoes
the language of the Liberalism then current. In later works,
such as *The Bible Today* ([1]1946; paperback, 1960) he puts
greater emphasis on God's initiative in revelation and on the
essential role of the Church as custodian and interpreter of the
Scriptures.

In the Bible, Dodd maintains, revelation is imparted historically, not merely in the sense that the prophets were progressively instructed in the word of God, but in the further sense
that the events themselves, in which the prophets were involved,
were revelatory. If it be objected that the prophetic interpretation is what makes the events revelatory, Dodd replies that
history never consists of naked, uninterpreted facts; "history
is occurrence *plus* meaning." The biblical revelation, while
including history, is supra-historical; for the meaning to which
the prophets bear witness comes from beyond all time. The
undying significance of the biblical events derives from the fact
that they stand at the intersection of eternity with time; hence
we can find in them God's word, the same yesterday, today, and
forever. Jesus Christ is the fulfilment of the history of Israel and
indeed of all history; he not only speaks the word of God; he is
that Word.

The divine dimension of salvation history, according to Dodd,
frees it from the limits of particularity by which it would otherwise be found. It gives us reason to believe that God reveals

35. One may conveniently use the paperback edition (New York, rev.,
[2]1962).

114

himself also to those who have not been evangelized concerning God's great deeds on behalf of his people. The gentiles, too,
stand under God's word of judgment and mercy.

4. RICHARDSON

Alan Richardson (1905–   ) studied at Liverpool and was
ordained an Anglican priest in 1929. He later did graduate work
in theology at Oxford, taught at the University of Nottingham,
and in 1964 became Dean of York. His views on revelation
are not dissimilar to those of Dodd. In *Christian Apologetics*[36]
he defends the view that there are two distinct types of revelation, general and special. General revelation is available through
the common religious experience of mankind, insofar as this
is illumined by God's gracious presence within the mind, of
which Augustine wrote so well. Special revelation, on the other
hand, depends upon God's action in a particular history—
that of the Israelites which reaches its consummation in Christ.
For practical purposes, special revelation corresponds to the
biblical religions. On the basis of this distinction Richardson
takes a stand against three positions which he considers unacceptable: that of the Thomists, who, as he thinks, hold that
all knowledge of God apart from historical revelation is merely
natural; that of the Liberals, who look upon the Israelite
prophets and Christ himself as religious geniuses, rather than
vessels of election; and the Barthian view, that would deny
any salvific value to the non-biblical religions.

With respect to the biblical revelation, Richardson criticizes
Temple for having erected a false dichotomy between facts and
interpretation. According to Richardson (who agrees at this
point with A. M. Ramsey and C. H. Dodd), we have no uninterpreted historical facts. We cannot measure the truth of
Christianity by its correspondence with bare facts, but only by
its capacity to give a full and coherent account of the evidences,
including the interpretations made by others. Christian faith,

36. London, 1947.

according to Richardson, can account for the faith of the early community, and is to that extent a reasonable position.

In *Christian Apologetics,* Richardson locates special revelation primarily in the prophets' inspired interpretation of the historical events in which they themselves were involved. This existential approach is further developed in *History Sacred and Profane* (1964). But in this later work Richardson shies away from traditional revelation language, and avoids any rigid line of demarcation between the biblical and other faiths. Borrowing a term from the linguistic philosopher, I. T. Ramsey,[37] Richardson speaks of "disclosure situations," by which he means moments of existential crisis in the life of an individual or of a nation, in which an illumination is given and a commitment called for.

The disclosure situations attested in the Old Testament are not different in kind from those of other histories. Their distinctive character consists in the depth of their penetration to that ultimate level where the nation, even one's own nation, is stripped of every pretence at self-justification and is brought to the recognition of basic moral values and of its own costly vocation to serve the righteousness of God in the midst of a concrete historical situation.[38]

For the Christian believer, Richardson maintains, the resurrection of Jesus has historical intelligibility insofar as it assigns an explanation for the faith of the early Christians and fits coherently into the general pattern of those disclosure situations by which Israel was progressively made aware of its special function in relation to God's universal salvific designs.

Richardson has developed many of the finest insights of Temple and Dodd, integrating them into a sophisticated theory of historiography. Some critics, however, feel uncomfortable at his reluctance to admit an objective order of facts to which sound interpretation must conform. His emphasis on the sub-

37. *Religious Language* (New York, 1957; paperback, 1963).
38. *History Sacred and Profane* (Philadelphia, 1964) 226.

jective sometimes conveys the impression of defiant irresponsibility.[39]

5. FARRER

Austin Farrer (1904–   ), an Anglo-Catholic theologian who served as chaplain of Trinity College at Oxford from 1935 to 1960, has long been a champion of Thomistic natural theology (*Finite and Infinite,* 1943). In his more recent works, however, he stresses that man's natural analogous knowledge of God is a mere preamble to a supernatural knowledge mediated by interpretative images. Holding that images are an irreducibly distinct medium of communication, Farrer maintains that revelation can never be adequately expressed in propositional language, whether this be historical and descriptive or doctrinal and abstract. The inspired biblical images have their basis in the archetypal images of the cosmic religions, but these images have been vastly enriched through the events of biblical history. This process of enrichment, begun in the Old Testament, was brought to completion by Christ and the apostles, through whom a "visible rebirth of images" was achieved.[40] The New Testament interprets the meaning of Christ's actions and sufferings through certain dominant images, such as the Kingdom of God, the Son of Man, and the Israel of God. "Faith discerns not the images, but what the images signify: and yet we cannot discern it except through the images. We cannot by-pass the images to seize an imageless truth."[41]

In various exegetical works on Mark, Matthew, and the Apocalypse, Farrer has sought to trace more precisely the symbolism of the New Testament. His hermeneutic methods have, however, been distressing to a number of critics, including Helen

39. See for instance the generally sympathetic criticisms in V. A. Harvey, *op. cit.,* 230–45. Also John Navone, *History and Faith in the Thought of Alan Richardson* (London, 1966).
40. *A Rebirth of Images* (Westminster, 1949) 14.
41. *The Glass of Vision* (London, 1948) 110.

Gardner, who objects that his style of typological exegesis is "too one-sided, too abstract, intellectual and bookish, too literary and aesthetic an approach to the interpretation of the Gospels."[42]

Farrer's fellow-Thomist, E. L. Mascall, in his *Words and Images* (1957) and in his *Theology and Images* (1963), has strongly endorsed Farrer's iconic approach to revelation. Alan Richardson, while generally agreeing, warns against Farrer's apparent tendency to equate the whole of revelation with inspired images:

The chief question in this field, with which theologians must occupy themselves in the immediate future, is that of the relation of the images to the biblical conception of the Word. Scripture says that the *Logos,* not the *eikon,* became flesh, and that the Word of the Lord, not the image, came to the prophets; Christian theology is a theology of the Word. When we understand the priority of the Word over the images, we shall see the matter in its right perspective.[43]

6. MACQUARRIE

One of the most articulate representatives of the *via media Anglicana* in contemporary theology is John Macquarrie (1919–   ), who, after studying at Glasgow and teaching there from 1953 to 1962, became professor of systematic theology at Union Theological Seminary in New York City. In his *Principles of Christian Theology* (1966) he synthesizes various insights from Rudolf Bultmann, Martin Heidegger, and Karl Rahner, achieving a theory of revelation which aims to be both authentically existential and soundly traditional.

Macquarrie distinguishes between two types of revelation. By primordial or classic revelation, he understands a definite disclosive experience of the holy which is paradigmatic for the

42. *The Business of Criticism* (Oxford, 1959) 154.
43. *The Bible in the Age of Science* (Philadelphia, 1961) 163.

subsequent experience of the holy within a given community. The subsequent reenactment of the disclosive experience within such a community Macquarrie calls "repetitive revelation." In his analysis of the experience of the holy, Macquarrie closely follows Rudolf Otto. The *mysterium tremendum et fascinans* is in Macquarrie's view the grasp of the transcendent (the wholly other) as gracious. Faith, which perceives being itself as gracious, is not the actuation of any universally accessible possibility, but rather a particular, concrete experience, which comes to the individual or to the community as a gift. Hence all revelation is "special"; there is no such thing as general revelation.

An experience *sui generis,* revelation, in Macquarrie's opinion, cannot properly be described in the categories of scientific knowledge. Science presupposes the subject-object distinction, which is overcome in revelation. The categories of personal knowledge are more appropriate; but revelation differs on so many counts from our knowledge of other human persons that not even an I-thou philosophy, such as Buber's, can provide an adequate framework. Heidegger's "foundational thinking," according to Macquarrie, provides the best philosophical analogue for revelation.

The content of revelation, Macquarrie maintains, is the dimension of depth found within the realities present to us in experience. Thus revelation has no particular content that can be directly expressed in verbal statements. It is rather the self-communication of Being itself, which seizes the whole of man and penetrates his entire life. But believers must make use of particular symbols in order to speak of the ways in which the divine has become manifest to them. Symbols drawn from personal life have the highest adequacy accessible to us. For Christians the supreme symbol of the Divine is the Incarnation, which they take to be the very revelation of God. The Christian creedal formulas point to the depth-dimension which constituted Jesus himself the primordial revelation for the infant Church, and which can be reappropriated by Christians of later generations through "repetitive thinking." The creeds and dogmas of the Church, while they must be reinterpreted, cannot be simply put aside without grave loss to the fullness of the faith.

Standing within the Anglican tradition, Macquarrie has enriched this with philosophical ideas derived from continental Europe. He provides a suitable bridge for a new approach to European theology, and more specifically, to the developments in Germany since Bultmann.

E. Biblical Theology and Salvation History

1. BIBLICAL THEOLOGY

Especially in continental Europe, biblical scholars of recent decades have been seriously concerned to anchor the theological conception of revelation more securely in the Bible. The great *Theologisches Wörterbuch zum Neuen Testament* (ET *Theological Dictionary of the New Testament*), which began to appear in 1933 under the general editorship of Gerhard Kittel —and which has been directed since Kittel's death by G. Friedrich—is a remarkably ambitious undertaking of this kind. Kittel and many of his colleagues have assumed that a painstaking analysis of the biblical vocabulary would yield some kind of authoritative theology of revelation. As Kittel stated in a lecture:

In the New Testament there are a large number of words used for the utterance of speech and the deliverance of a message. . . . These words . . . are bound up inextricably with a definite historical fact to which they bear witness. . . . The language of the New Testament has quite definitely but one single purpose, that of expressing that which has taken place, that which God has done in Christ. New Testament words are thus essentially like a mirror; they reflect the fact of Christ, and this they do not in any broken or indirect way, but in actual reality and in genuine truth. . . . For the words and sentences in which the message is framed are formed by men who are imbued with the fact of Christ. They never speak in order to

120

communicate their own wisdom or any theological or philosophical ideas.[44]

Many of the contributors to the *Wörterbuch* have shared Kittel's conviction that the very words used by the biblical writers are direct reflections of revelation through historical events. For example, A. Oepke in his article, *apokalyptō,* after quoting several passages from Isaiah and Psalms, goes on to say:

Here at once we see the nature of revelation on the OT view. Revelation is not the impartation of supernatural knowledge or the excitement of numinous feelings. Knowledge can certainly come through revelation, and the revelation of God will be accompanied by numinuos feelings (Ex. 19:16; Is. 6:5; and so forth). But revelation is not to be identified with these. In the proper sense, it is the action of Yahweh. It is the removal of his essential concealment, his self-offering for fellowship. The distinctive feature of this fellowship, moreover, is that it rests on a moral foundation.[45]

Similarly, O. Procksch, in his article, *logos* (IV, pp. 91–100), finds that the word of God in the Old Testament is not a mere *flatus vocis* but a dynamic embodiment of the speaker's own personality. The word of Yahweh, heralded by the prophet or other charismatic emissary, effectively brings about that which it announces. As J. L. McKenzie, in a summary presentation of this point of view, puts it: "The word of Yahweh, like the word of man, is a release of the power of the personality which utters it. He who receives the word is invaded by the personality of the speaker; when the speaker is Yahweh, the transforming influence of the word exceeds the influence of any human speech."[46]

44. G. Kittel, *Lexiocographia Sacra* (London, 1938); quoted by James Barr, *The Semantics of Biblical Language* (London, 1961) 207–208.
45. Article "Kalyptō," and so forth, in *Theological Dictionary of the New Testament* 3 (Grand Rapids, 1965) 573.
46. J. L. McKenzie, "The Word of God in the Old Testament," *Theological Studies* 21 (1960) 195; reprinted in his *Myths and Realities* (Milwaukee, 1963) 37–58.

Generalizations such as this are likely to leave the reader uneasy on several counts. For one thing, he might wonder whether, if the Bible accepts this view of the word, this might not be an instance of primitive or mythical thinking, which the contemporary critical student should "demythologize." Furthermore, it may be questioned whether this dynamic conception of revelation is adequately supported by impartial biblical scholarship. The capable Scottish exegete, James Barr, takes the view that the theologians of the *Wörterbuch* vintage are far more influenced by the theology of the word that developed in the 1930's and 1940's than by a sheerly lexical study of the biblical terms. In *The Semantics of Biblical Language* (1961) Barr argues that it is illegitimate to infer from the ambiguity in the Hebrew term *dabar* (word, thing) that the ancient Semites accepted the dynamic efficacy of the word. Elsewhere he contests the biblical warrant for the common view that God reveals himself in and through history. "Not a single case exists for a use of the word 'reveal' for the events of Exodus and Mount Sinai."[47]

Barr is careful to explain that he is not seeking to banish the idea of revelation through history. He feels obliged, however, to point out that God, in the biblical view, can impart specific verbal messages, when he so wills, to the men of his choice. "If we persist in saying that this direct, specific communication must be subsumed under revelation through events in history and taken as subsidiary interpretation of the latter, I shall say that we are abandoning the Bible's own representation of the matter for another which is apologetically more comfortable."[48]

Barr's contentions, if they are well founded, would seem to weaken the central thesis of Harvard's biblical archaeologist, G. Ernest Wright, in his provocative little book, *God Who Acts*. "Biblical theology," according to Wright, "is the confessional recital of the redemptive acts of God in a particular history, be-

47. Article "Revelation" in J. Hastings, *Dictionary of the Bible* (New York, rev., 1963) 847–49.
48. "Revelation Through History in the Old Testament and in Modern Theology," *New Theology* 1 (New York, 1964) 60–74, especially 70.

cause history is the chief medium of revelation."[49] "It is thus evident that the core of the Old Testament was a proclamation, a kerygma, of the great saving acts of God which brought Israel into being, in the light of which the subsequent history of the nation was compiled."[50] Following the Heidelberg scholar, Gerhard von Rad, Wright calls particular attention to the solemn confessions recalling the Exodus and the Conquest of Canaan. In his antipathy to abstract doctrinal formulations, Wright seems to take the position that revelation originally consisted in deeds alone, and that God's action in history is in principle a sufficient communication of what he has to say.[51]

Two of the leading European biblical theologians, Gerhard von Rad and Walther Eichrodt, while agreeing as to the primarily historical character of revelation, have recently espoused differing views as to the importance of the factual basis of the kerygmatic history contained in the Old Testament. Von Rad seems to hold, somewhat as Bultmann does for the New Testament, that what matters is the existential understanding of the individual believer, rather than the relationship between that understanding and any real events.[52] Eichrodt, on the other hand, insists that the Old Testament must be accepted as an accurate presentation of God's sovereign control over the course of events. "The link between the testimony of faith and the facts of history is not therefore a topic to be excluded from the scope of Old Testament theology, but calls for continuous and careful attention."[53]

2. CULLMANN

Born in Strasbourg in 1902, Oscar Cullmann first became prominent in 1925, when he published an important article on form

49. *God Who Acts* (*Studies in Biblical Theology* 8) (London, 1952) 13.
50. *Ibid.*, 76.
51. Cf. *ibid.*, 44.
52. For von Rad's views on the discrepancy between the historical events themselves and their kerygmatic presentation see his *Old Testament Theology* 1 (New York, 1962) 105–28.
53. *Theology of the Old Testament* 1 (Philadelphia, 1961) 516–17.

criticism. Since 1927 he has taught New Testament and early church history at Strasbourg, Basel, and Paris, and has been a visiting professor in the United States and elsewhere. A layman, he holds membership in both the Lutheran and Reformed churches. His thought on revelation is chiefly contained in *Christ and Time* (1946; ET 1951) and *Salvation in History* (1965; ET 1967).

Cullmann builds his theology about a theory of *Heilsgeschichte* which he took over, with significant modifications, from J. C. K. Hofmann (1810–77) and the Erlangen school. He holds that the Biblical revelation has as its primary theme God's redemptive action in history. Even God is not an object of revelation except in function of his salvific activity. The Bible tells the story of God's redemptive dealings with his elect people —a story that progressively narrows down to focus on Christ as the representative of mankind, and then expands from Pentecost, as the message of salvation is carried out to the ends of the earth.

In focussing on redemptive history as the chief content of revelation, Cullmann opposes the Rationalists, who conceive of revelation as timeless truth; the Barthians, who take refuge in primal history or metahistory (*Urgeschichte* and *Uebergeschichte*); and the Bultmannians, who tend to separate faith from belief in past historical occurrences. To some extent, Cullmann has come into conflict with Catholic theologians, who hold that church dogmas concerning the divine essence and persons are—in regard to their content—non-temporal and yet revealed. For Cullmann these dogmas are a correct and necessary inference from the Bible, but are not themselves revealed.

When he speaks of the relationship between secular and sacred history, Cullmann notes that the biblical writers make a very definite selection of the events and view them in relationship to an eschatological consummation which is knowable only by revelation. The Bible therefore gives us not ordinary history, but rather "revealed prophecy concerning history."[54]

54. *Christ and Time* (Philadelphia, [3]1964) 98.

Cullmann has brilliantly synthesized a vast number of biblical materials into a pattern that is simple, comprehensive, and enlightening. But his antiphilosophical bias has thus far prevented him from giving a coherent justification of his principles and procedures. He seems to take it for granted that the modern Christian is bound to accept the views of the biblical writers regarding time and history, and that philosophical reflection cannot possibly improve on the biblical outlook. Although he has written at length on the relationship between event and interpretation in the biblical revelation,[55] he has failed to make it clear, in the opinion of many critics, why the biblical events and no others form the line of redemptive history from Adam to Christ. He has given no explanation of how either the events themselves or the prophetic interpretations of them achieve the status of revelation.[56] The exegetical data assembled by Cullmann, however, give valuable confirmation of the systematic insights of theologians such as Richardson and Pannenberg, who likewise emphasize the historical dimension of revelation.

F. New Trends in Swiss and German Theology

1. THE INFLUENCE OF THE LATER HEIDEGGER

As we have already seen, Bultmann's existential theology of revelation was heavily influenced by the early work of Martin Heidegger (1889–   ). But Heidegger himself gradually took what many regard as a decisive turn from existential to ontological thinking.[57] Much of his published work since World War II takes the form of a meditation on the givenness of being. Being, he finds, reveals itself as "*alētheia*" (unveiledness, truth) in the

---

55. Cf. *Salvation in History* (New York, 1967) 133–66.
56. See for instance the critique in J. Macquarrie, *The Scope of Demythologizing* (*op. cit.*) 62–64.
57. See W. J. Richardson, *Heidegger: Through Phenomenology to Thought* (The Hague, 1963); also W. J. Richardson, "Heidegger and Theology," *Theological Studies* 26 (1965) 86–100.

particular beings we know from experience; but because no being is Being itself, Being may be said also to hide itself in beings. In search of Being, then, the philosopher must interrogate beings, not simply to note what they reveal but also to discover what they conceal.

Heidegger achieved another crucial insight when he perceived that being manifests itself through language. Man, he now holds, is the place where being's voice is heard. Since this discovery Heidegger has proceeded on the assumption that the highway to Being lies through meditation on the language of those writers—philosophers and especially poets—in whom being has come to expression. His philosophy takes the form of hermeneutics, and his hermeneutics is oriented to ontology.

Although Heidegger does not consider himself a theologian (and has been thought by some to be an atheist), we have already seen how a theologian such as Macquarrie can draw on him for the theology of revelation. The young Swiss Reformed theologian, Heinrich Ott (1929–   ), who worked closely under Barth at Basel, has sought to use the later Heidegger as a catalyst to bring Barth and Bultmann into closer agreement. He advocates that both should address themselves to the themes which Heidegger has recently been developing.

In particular, Ott makes use of Heidegger's philosophy of language and of his hermeneutical theory for grounding the principles of exegesis. The theme of theology, Ott believes, is not the words of Scripture but the revealing God who partly discloses and partly conceals himself in the words of his human witnesses. "Each individual Biblical witness has his own specific 'unspoken poem,' out of which he speaks. And also all Biblical witnesses together have the same 'unspoken poem' out of which they bear witness. It is one and the same subject matter, which is not *intended* by them but which *inspires* them all and sets in motion their thinking and speaking, namely God in his revelation."[58]

58. H. Ott, "Response," in J. M. Robinson and J. B. Cobb, Jr. (eds.), *The Later Heidegger and Theology* (New York, 1963) 205–06.

Several German theologians of the Bultmann circle, influenced by the later Heidegger and his disciple Gadamer, hold that revelation is essentially a language event. They argue that the word which came to expression in Christ, and is preserved for us in the Bible, becomes a living word for us as we interpret Scripture with a view to proclamation.

Ernst Fuchs (1903–), a former pupil of Bultmann, who has successively taught at Tübingen, Berlin, and Marburg, sets forth a theology of revelation based on the Heideggerian thesis that reality is essentially linguistic.[59] By this he means that in every event being comes to expression in a meaningful way, and is tending to become fully articulate. Revelation, for Fuchs, is the language event (*Sprachereignis*) of God's word admitting one to authentic existence. The supreme event in which God himself came definitively to human language was the preaching of Jesus. In the New Testament, not only the words of Jesus, but the entire story of his life, death, and resurrection has been raised to the level of language. The language event of the New Testament has been reenacted through the centuries in Christian proclamation, whereby the body of Christ is assembled. In such proclamation, "God's revelation comes to encounter precisely as present insofar as God is present in a word."[60] Thus the word of revelation brings history to a close. When it occurs, there is no longer past or future, but only present.

A highly original and creative thinker, Fuchs writes in a style which many find murky. He has been severely criticized for his obscurity by those who value clarity and system. Others complain that he so concentrates on revelation as encounter and decision that he unduly neglects content; revelation, for him, reveals nothing. It is likewise objected that Fuchs overplays the role of present experience to the detriment of the saving oc-

59. G. C. O'Collins. "Reality as Language: Ernst Fuchs's Theology of Revelation," *Theological Studies* 28 (1967) 76–93.
60. "Das Fest der Verlorenen" in E. Fuchs, *Glaube und Erfahrung* (Gesammelte Aufsätze 3) (Tübingen, 1965) 411.

currences in the past and the eschatological hope reserved for the future.[61]

Fuchs' closest associate in the new hermeneutical theology has been Gerhard Ebeling (1912–   ), who was Fuchs' colleague at Tübingen after World War II, and who, after ten years' teaching at Zurich, returned to teach again at Tübingen. Ebeling started as a church historian, and in this capacity became convinced that church history is nothing but the history of the interpretation of Holy Scripture. Since then, Ebeling has moved into the fields of fundamental theology and dogmatics. He now understands the whole of theology as hermeneutics.

Revelation, according to Ebeling, is not primarily Holy Scripture nor is it primarily the disclosure of general timeless truths. Rather, it is the concrete and unique event of the appearance of Jesus Christ. But this event, although attested as past occurrence, has an abiding present quality insofar as Jesus "is proclaimed as the present Lord exalted to the right hand of God" and insofar as his death and exaltation are still heralded as the message of salvation.[62] The word of God, having entered history in Jesus, continues to shape its course. The task of the Church, in which the theologian must assist, is to bring the word of God to expression for each successive historical era.

Ebeling, with his more systematic style of thought and writing, and with his mastery of historical theology, has done much to refine and disseminate the ideas of his more intuitive colleague, Ernst Fuchs.

2. PANNENBERG

Wolfhart Pannenberg (1928–   ), before engaging in theology, studied philosophy under Nicolai Hartmann and Karl Jaspers.

61. See the criticisms of Amos Wilder and others in J. M. Robinson and J. B. Cobb, Jr. (eds.), *The New Hermeneutic* (New York, 1964).
62. *Word and Faith* (Philadelphia, 1963) 29.

When he came to Heidelberg as a student in 1951, he continued his philosophical studies under Karl Löwith while doing systematic theology under Edmund Schlink and Peter Brunner, and biblical studies under Gerhard von Rad, among others. While at Heidelberg he became the leader of a small circle of graduate students in various branches of theology (biblical, historical, systematic, and practical), who have continued to collaborate, especially in examining the theological conception of history. After a period at Wüppertal, until 1961, he taught at Mainz until the end of 1967, and then joined the new Evangelical faculty at Munich. He became internationally prominent when he and his "working circle" published a programmatic symposium, *Revelation as History*.[63] His more recent views are set forth in his essay, "The Revelation of God in Jesus of Nazareth."[64]

Like Cullmann, Pannenberg stresses revelation through the deeds of God in history, as interpreted by a constantly developing tradition. But he criticizes Cullmann for apparently holding that the interpretation of salvation history is something independent of the events, added on, as it were, from the outside by an authoritative word. In opposition to all word-theologies, including those of Barth, Bultmann, and their disciples, Pannenberg holds that words have no revelatory value beyond their power to express the meaning that is intrinsic to the events themselves, provided these are viewed in their full historical context.

Modern man, trained in the realism of Feuerbach and Freud, can no longer, in Pannenberg's opinion, accept any claim of revelation that cannot be critically tested. The Old Testament theophanies, while they may have conveyed revelation to the ancient Israelites, are no longer valid as revelation for us. The words of the prophets have value insofar as they point to, and are confirmed by, the deeds God was to accomplish. Since by

63. Göttingen, [1]1961; ET, New York, 1968.
64. J. M. Robinson and J. B. Cobb, Jr. (eds.), *Theology as History* (New York, 1967) 101–133. See also Pannenberg's response to the discussion, 221–76.

God we understand the one who has power over everything, the only true test of divinity is universal history.

Does this mean for Pannenberg that there will be no full revelation until history comes to a close? In a sense, yes. But Pannenberg adds that in the life of Jesus, and especially in his resurrection, the eschatological consummation became proleptically present. Faith discerns the meaning of the resurrection as the anticipation of the final consummation, and is therefore able to cling to God in absolute trust. In Jesus Christ, therefore, we have the final, though still anticipatory, revelation of God. The history of Jesus, says Pannenberg, is the event uniting and reconciling all other events to the whole, and is thus the key to the meaning of all history, both human and cosmic.

In his systematic study, *Jesus—God and Man* (German [1]1964; ET 1968), Pannenberg presents his case for a revelationally centered Christology. After paying tribute to Barth for having evolved a presentation of Christ's divinity on the basis of the concept of God's revelation in Jesus, Pannenberg adds:

The idea of the revelatory presence of God in Jesus, of a revelatory identity between Jesus and God, which includes identity of essence, will prove more and more clearly in the course of our discussions to be the only appropriate understanding of the presence of God in Jesus. . . . The patristic idea of a substantial presence of God in Jesus has become accessible in our century from the perspective of the problem of revelation, insofar as revelation implies identity of essence.[65]

Pannenberg seems to be justified in his complaint that modern revelational theology, especially in the Barthian tradition, has been too fideistic and esoteric. Falling back on a peculiar "blik" or perspectival view, it has relinquished the standpoint of universal reason to unbelievers. In place of this cloistered attitude Pannenberg proposes a bold and impressive synthesis of biblical faith with cosmic history. In affirming that revelation *is* history,

65. *Jesus—God and Man* (Philadelphia, 1968) 132.

he commits himself to a very wide notion of historical method, unacceptable to many professonal historians. Once this comprehensive notion of history is broken down into its various components, it may turn out that Pannenberg will be forced back into many of the traditional distinctions he has been inclined to question—such as those between fact and interpretation, salvation history and world history, reason and revelation. But his stress on the ultimate unity of knowledge, and on the coherence between the immanent goal of history and eschatological salvation, has done much to offset the dichotomous antitheses that have plagued theology since the Cartesian era. Pannenberg's own competence in exegesis, historical theology, and philosophy, plus the support of a strong team of theological associates, makes his point of view an exciting alternative to the word-theology of the Bultmannians.

3. MOLTMANN

Jürgen Moltmann (1926–   ), an Evangelical Reformed theologian who received his doctorate from Göttingen University in 1957, has taught at Wüppertal, at Bonn, and, since 1968, at Tübingen. His *Theology of Hope* (German, 1965; ET 1967), like Pannenberg's work, sets forth a theology of revelation heavily influenced by Hegel. In line with the Reformed tradition (and notably Calvin himself), Moltmann understands promise rather than history as the correlative of faith. He questions the desirability of starting out with a formal conception of revelation, such as the disclosure of that which is normally hidden. This view of revelation, too hastily applied to Christianity, tends to force biblical faith into a class with the pagan epiphany religions. The distinctive note of Israelite faith, according to Moltmann, is its denial that this world is capable of becoming transparent to the divine. In the biblical view, therefore, the question of revelation can bear only on the problem when and where the God of promise reveals his faithfulness.

On this basis Moltmann proceeds to criticize the revelational

131

theology of the past century. Dominated by Kantian philosophy, he maintains, Herrmann, Barth, and Bultmann were incapable of conceiving revelation as the opening up of the future in terms of promise, but only as the coming of the eternal to man, or as man's coming to himself. Revelation for these theologians becomes the apocalypse of the transcendent subjectivity of God or of man. Redemption, then, could only mean deliverance from the confines of this world and through union with the transcendent. An authentic Christian eschatology, on the contrary, demands that the world itself be seen as radically open to transformation by the God of promise.

In the theologies of salvation history, especially in Pannenberg, Moltmann finds laudable efforts to free theology from the fetters of transcendental subjectivity. But Pannenberg seems to neglect the spiritual situation of our age in imagining that, for our society, revelation could manifest and verify itself as history. Rather, revelation should disclose to that society for the first time the eschatological goal of history. "The theologian is not concerned merely to supply a different *interpretation* of the world, of history, and of human nature, but to *transform* them in expectation of a divine transformation."[66] Theology must apprehend the world as threatened by death and as subjected to vanity before it can direct the world to the promised future of God.

In answer to this critique, Pannenberg complains that Moltmann has at many points misunderstood and misrepresented his positions.[67] He insists, however, that the past occurrence of the resurrection in Jesus Christ sets Christianity far apart from the theologies which, like Judaism, live off a totally futurist eschatology. It would seem that Moltmann's theology of promise and hope has something to learn from Pannenberg's emphasis on historical facts as revelation. Because Pannenberg insists that the resurrection of Jesus is only a proleptic realization of the

66. *Theology of Hope* (London, 1967) 84.
67. W. Pannenberg, "Response to the Discussion," *Theology as History,* especially 250–66.

eschaton, he can make ample room for many of Moltmann's insights regarding openness toward the future.

G. The Deflation of Revelation

This chapter will conclude on a descending note, which is, however, in basic harmony with the tendencies already noted in authors such as Barr, Pannenberg, and Moltmann. During the past generation an increasing number of capable theologians in the Anglican and Protestant traditions have become convinced that the theology of the word, especially in Karl Barth, has resulted in what the Lutheran Paul Althaus, a generation ago, labelled "the inflation of the concept of revelation."[68]

Dietrich Bonhoeffer (1906–45) gave impetus to this trend by accusing Barth of "revelational positivism."[69] Barth, he protested, presented Christianity in a dogmatic way that left modern man with no choice but to "take it or leave it." After committing himself to accept revelation, Barth proceeded to talk about God and his attributes in a way that Bonhoeffer regarded as excessively facile and uncritical. Bonhoeffer felt that theology should be more modest in its claims and more ready to engage in dialogue with modern secular man. The radical theologians of the 1960's (including William Hamilton, Paul van Buren, and Harvey Cox) commonly appeal to Bonhoeffer as an authority for their reticence in speaking of God, revelation, and dogma.

Some of the more traditional theologians share with the radicals a certain uneasiness regarding modern Protestantism's preoccupation with the theme of revelation. The Anglican, F. Gerald Downing, in his *Has Christianity a Revelation?*, contends that the term "revelation" is pretentious and confusing. While there seems to be a rather general consensus among twentieth-century theologians regarding the centrality of revelation, the

68. Paul Althaus, "Die Inflation des Begriffs der Offenbarung in der gegenwärtigen Theologie," *Zeitschrift für systematische Theologie* 18 (1941) 134–49.

69. *Letters and Papers from Prison* (New York, paperback, rev., 1967) 144, 170–72.

agreement is more verbal than real, because the theologians in question use the term in vastly different senses (for example, as propositional truths, as existential encounter, and so forth). The term, moreover, is misleading because it suggests a clarity of manifestation which is not vouchsafed to the Christian believer. To become meaningful in theology, the word "revelation" has to be extensively qualified—a confusion that could have been avoided by adoption of some other term.

Appealing to scholars such as James Barr,[70] Downing contends that the Bible itself does not use the word "revelation," as modern theologians do, to designate God's action in Jesus Christ. For the New Testament writers, he holds, God remains quite hidden in his saving activity. "Once a predominant stress on revelation has been removed, a full and largely traditional theology may be stated and even defended, and perhaps lived."[71] Seeking to do better justice to the full richness of Christian life and faith, Downing proposes substituting "salvation" for "revelation" as the central theological concept.

The American Lutheran, Carl E. Braaten (1929–   ), takes a somewhat similar position. The dominant emphasis on revelation in modern Protestant theology, he observes, reflects the heightened epistemological consciousness that was introduced into theology by Kant's critical philosophy. When the problem of religious knowledge becomes central, the idea of revelation moves to the center of the stage. Barthian theology, while pretending to be totally theocentric, actually revolves about the dilemmas of contemporary secular man. Accepting the radical agnosticism of the unbelieving world, Barth erects the knowledge of God solely on revelation, received in an act of faith which claims to be its own justification. "If this is the best that theology can do today, it ought at least to be acknowledged as a new, and rather desperate, apologetic maneuver of church theology in the face of an embarrassment."[72] While Braaten is

70. See above, p. 122.
71. *Has Christianity a Revelation?* (London, 1964) 240.
72. *History and Hermeneutics* (*New Directions in Theology Today* 2) (Philadelphia, 1966) 13.

far from rejecting the notion of revelation, he believes that it would be more faithful to the Bible and more consonant with the Christian reality to take reconciliation rather than revelation as the focal concept for theology.

To all these authors we may concede that the unprecedented emphasis on revelation in modern Protestant theology is partly due to the hypertrophy of the epistemological problem, especially since Kant. This emphasis, carried to an extreme, can be dangerous. In combination with the traditional dichotomy between faith and reason, an exaltation of revelation tends to isolate believers in a private world of their own and to impede communications between them and the rest of humanity. Christianity itself, moreover, loses much of its impact if it is conceived in an excessively cerebral manner. Under the quasi-magisterium of university professors, some branches of Protestantism have tended to look upon salvation as if it were simply a matter of thinking and knowing, rather than of total transformation through God's self-giving in Jesus Christ.

On the other hand, it would be regrettable if theologians, reacting against admitted exaggerations, were to neglect the singular way in which God has made himself known through the prophets, Christ, and the Church. In the Introduction to this survey we have already seen that the self-communication of God, to which the Church bears witness, is of constitutive importance for theology and for the whole Christian life. While revelation is not the sum and substance of Christianity, it has a certain logical priority in the Christian scheme of things.

5. CATHOLIC THEOLOGY SINCE 1910

The problematic of the Catholic theology of revelation for the twentieth century has thus far remained, in substance, that set by the Modernist movement. Though condemned by the Encyclical of 1907, the shades of the movement continued to haunt the Catholic theological consciousness for the next fifty years and more. For Modernism had correctly identified the most pressing issue facing the Church: how to reconcile the Catholic understanding of revelation with openness to the modern world? The modern consciousness calls for the autonomy of science; it is acutely sensitive to historical change, and it esteems the creativity of the human spirit. The standard doctrine of revelation, as set forth in Catholic theology since the middle ages, insisted on the hegemony of the Church over the human sciences, the permanence and stability of revealed truth, and man's obligation to submit humbly before the word of God, as something delivered from outside, sealed by miraculous guarantees. While Modernism embraced, or at least dallied with, naturalism, transformism, and immanentism, Catholic theology in the anti-Modernist period insisted more vehemently than ever before on supernaturalism, irreformability, and transcendence.

A. The Latin Manuals

The Catholic reply to Modernism was to a great extent developed in the Latin manuals, which dominated the theology

136

of revelation in seminary teaching throughout the first half of the twentieth century.

Christian Pesch, S.J., (1853–1925), professor at the German theologate at Valkenburg in Holland, followed with great precision and clarity the principles of Suarez and de Lugo. In the first volume of his nine-volume *Praelectiones Dogmaticae* (1894–99),[1] he distinguishes between natural revelation, which is made through the works of creation, and supernatural revelation, "whereby God manifests his mind in a manner beyond the order of nature." Natural revelation, says Pesch, is communicated by realities (*per facta*), supernatural revelation by words. Whereas deeds are suited to manifest impersonal things, words are capable of manifesting the person.

Hermann Dieckmann, S.J., who was also a member of the Valkenburg faculty, published his manual *De revelatione christiana* in 1930. He sets forth a collection of definitions, culled from manuals of the period, and remarks that there is no great difference among them. He himself settles on the brief definition of van Laak, "locutio Dei attestans," and then proceeds to elaborate this in terms of the classical four causes of Aristotelian scholasticism.[2] A similar collection of definitions and divisions may be found in the article on Revelation in the *Dictionnaire de théologie catholique* by N. Iung, S.J., who accepts the brief definition, "the word of God teaching and attesting."[3]

Among the manualists of the period, special mention should be made of Réginald Garrigou-Lagrange, O.P. (1877–1964). After studying and teaching at the Dominican house of studies of the Paris Province, then located at Le Saulchoir in Belgium, Garrigou-Lagrange was transferred to the Angelicum in Rome, where he continued to teach until 1960 and where he exerted great influence in favor of systematic neo-Thomism. Compared

1. *Institutiones propadeuticae ad sacram theologiam* (Freiburg im Br., ⁷1924) especially no. 151, pp. 112–13.
2. *De revelatione christiana* (Freiburg im Br., 1930), nos. 193–220, pp. 134–56.
3. *Dictionnaire de théologie catholique* 13/2 (Paris, 1937) cols. 2580–2618.

with other manuals of the day, his *De revelatione per Ecclesiam Catholicam proposita*[4] gives a remarkably ample and positive discussion of the nature of revelation. His definition follows the pattern of the traditional four causes:

Revelation is the free and essentially supernatural action by which God, in order to lead the human race to its supernatural end, which consists in the vision of the divine essence, speaking to us through the prophets and finally through Christ, has manifested to us in a kind of darkness supernatural mysteries and natural truths of religion, in such wise that they might thenceforth be proposed infallibly by the Church, without any change of significance even to the end of the world.[5]

In his discussion of revelation, Garrigou-Lagrange distinguishes sharply between revelation itself, which he regards as an objectively given word of God "in the form of teaching," and the subjective, supernatural light, which he maintains is required for the believer to make a salutary act of faith.

These definitions and distinctions seem in a way almost self-evident, but from another point of view they are quite unsatisfactory. In recent years it has become common to attack them as abstract, static, and formalistic. As Werner Bulst, S.J. remarks:

The emphasis of these theologians is almost always on making an exclusively rational analysis of the concept of revelation; this is especially evident in Dieckmann and Garrigou-Lagrange. The Scriptures serve only as the point of departure for the analysis or to provide proof texts, which in turn—as in Tanquerey—frequently appear only in footnotes.[6]

A more searching analysis of the biblical testimonies would have enabled these authors to give a far more dynamic, concrete, and personal notion of revelation, and to do better justice

4. Rome, 2 vols.; [1]1918.
5. Rome, [4]1945; vol. 1, 132.
6. W. Bulst, *Revelation* (New York, 1965) 22.

to the role of the events of salvation history in manifesting the powerful mercies of God. In the words of Roger Aubert:

Revelation has too often been conceived as a communication by God of a certain number of disconcerting statements which men must hold true without understanding them. Actually, revelation is presented by Scripture in a far less notional and more personal manner: it is above all the manifestation of God himself, who, through a sacred history, culminating in the death and resurrection of Christ, enables us to glimpse the mystery of his love.[7]

B. Speculative Theology in France and Belgium

1. THE SAULCHOIR DOMINICANS

Garrigou-Lagrange's theological professor, Ambroise Gardeil, O.P. (1859–1931), who served from 1897 to 1912 as regent of studies at Le Saulchoir, strove systematically to construct an orthodox notion of revelation that could stand up under any criticism which the Modernists might direct at it. One of his most important books, *Le donné révélé et la théologie* (1909),[8] was concerned with the problem how the content of revelation, although expressed in human concepts and words, could have permanent and universal validity. For his solution he relied principally on the treatise on prophecy in the *Summa theologica* of St. Thomas. He maintained that the prophet was not a principal cause, but a mere instrument of God, and that God elevated the consciousness of the prophet by a supernatural charism, given for the benefit of the whole Church. Under the influence of this charism, the prophet's mind produced new images, or rearranged the images already accumulated from experience, and thus generated appropriate concepts. More importantly still, the prophet was able to judge by an infused light and thus to affirm with divine certitude realities that lay

7. "Questioni attuali intorno all'atto di fede," *Problemi e Orientamenti di Teologia Dommatica* 2 (Milan, 1957) 671.
8. Paris, ²1932.

beyond his natural capacities. The divine influence, moreover, guaranteed the process by which the affirmation came to expression, and thus assured that the formulas would be appropriate to transmit the revealed datum to others.

Having thus described the original process of revelation, Gardeil in the remainder of his book addressed himself to the problems how the revealed data become translated into those technical official utterances of the Church which we call dogmas, and how dogmas can develop in the course of time without prejudice to the permanence and sufficiency of the faith once and for all delivered to the saints.

Gardeil wrote in a calm, dispassionate style, and set forth his arguments with extraordinary lucidity. But it may be objected that he was too little concerned with the actual process by which revelation was imparted in biblical times. His abstract, conceptual presentation of revelation seems almost out of contact with the vibrant realities of Christian faith.

Gardeil's disciple, M. D. Chenu (1895–   ), who succeeded him as regent of studies at Le Saulchoir and held that office from 1928 to 1942, skillfully probed the implications of Gardeil's position regarding the role of supernatural interior illumination in the act of faith. Relying chiefly on St. Thomas, but drawing inspiration at the same time from the Catholic Tübingen theologians of the nineteenth century, Chenu concluded that in faith we adhere not simply to God's message, but to God as he makes himself present and bears witness to himself by his gracious indwelling:

The act of the believer terminates, truthfully speaking, not in the dogmatic statement, but in the divine reality itself, which the proposition expresses in human terms. Its object, then, is not a concept, formula, or system of thought, but the Person in whom I recognize the All of my life, the satisfying object of my blessedness. Faith is, to be sure, an assent to propositions, as authentic vehicles of its religious perception; but that is its misery, or rather the provisional weakness of my mind, which does not know truth, even divine truth, except in propositions. But faith is, beyond this, and thanks to this, adherence to that which satisfies all desires, the sole desire of my soul: beatitude in the gift of God himself.[9]

Chenu, then, took a concrete and realist approach to revelation as the primary content of faith. While the datum of faith, in his opinion, was received from outside, it did not remain external to us. God, in giving himself through the statements of faith, becomes more interior to us than we to ourselves. Seeking to overcome the aridity and abstractness of the usual Scholastic analyses of revelation, Chenu stressed, far more than Garrigou-Lagrange or Gardeil, the concrete realities of salvation history as proclaimed in the Bible. Objecting to those authors who turned to the sources only for proofs and confirmation of what they already maintained on systematic grounds, Chenu insisted that we should listen to the Bible and to tradition with docility.

Chenu's little study of theology at Le Saulchoir was placed on the Index in 1942, for reasons not made public. Perhaps it seemed to the authorities of time that his views were dangerously close to those of the Modernists. However that may be, Chenu is to be praised as one of the thinkers who helped to liberate the Catholic theology of revelation from the sterile conceptualism into which it had fallen.

Closely associated with Chenu was his fellow Dominican, L. Charlier, whose *Essai sur le problème théologique* (1938) was also placed on the Index in 1942. While praising Gardeil for having restored the primacy of the revealed datum in theology, Charlier felt that Gardeil had dwelt too much on the conceptual and not sufficiently on the real element. "Our divine faith," he wrote, "is not a mere adherence to some kind of external divine testimony, a word guaranteed by God. The analogy drawn from human faith is on this point very deficient. Faith is assimilation to the first Truth (*veritas prima in dicendo*). To adhere to the first Truth in itself and for itself is to adhere to God in his

9. *La Foi dans l'intelligence* (Paris, 1964) 250; reprinted from his earlier book, *La théologie au Saulchoir* (Paris, 1937).

mystery, to attain him directly, and to grasp him in his intimate being and life."[10]

As Latourelle recognizes,[11] Charlier's book, despite its condemnation by Rome, contains precious elements that should find a place in any valid theology of revelation—the realism of God's self-manifestation, its progressive and historical character, and its interpersonal, gratuitous nature as a divine gift of love.

The school of Le Saulchoir, under the capable direction of Gardeil and Chenu, made a contribution of unique value. In place of the desiccated Scholasticism prevalent in other theological centers, it offered a more dynamic and authentic Thomism, capable of entering into dialogue with modern thought. The great ecclesiologist and ecumenist, Yves Congar, O.P., studied at Le Saulchoir and taught there in the years preceding World War II.

2. FRENCH AND BELGIAN JESUITS

The Thomism of Gardeil, and *a fortiori* that of Chenu and Charlier, by focussing on the active role of the intellect and on the inner attraction of grace in the communication of revealed truth, converged in some ways with the philosophical orientations of the French Jesuit, Pierre Rousselot (1878–1915) and of his Belgian confrère, Joseph Maréchal (1878–1944). Relying on St. Thomas, but exploiting also certain insights of Kant, Newman, and Blondel, they stressed the subjectivity of the human spirit in the process of knowing. Truth, for them, was not passively imposed on the intellect from outside, like a photograph on a film, but was achieved by the synthesizing intervention of the agent intellect. The absolute value of human knowledge, for both these philosophers, is attributable to the dynamic thrust of the mind toward the Infinite. Thanks to this dynamism, man can apprehend reality

10. *Essai sur le problème théologique* (Thuilles, Belgium, 1938) 66.
11. *Theology of Revelation* (*op. cit.*) 221.

from an absolute point of view. The human affirmation, more-over, never stops at propositions but passes through them to the real. Thus the active tendency of the intellect, in faith, termi-nates in God himself rather than in mere statements about God.

These epistemological positions, especially as applied to the act of faith, had important implications for the theology of revelation. As Rousselot showed,[12] the epistemology here in question, when brought to bear on the assent of faith, implies that the human spirit must be inwardly transformed and attuned to the divine by the grace of faith itself.

Maréchal's colleague at Louvain, Emile Mersch, S.J. (1890–1940), in his *Theology of the Mystical Body* (published posthumously, 1944), adumbrated an extraordinarily rich, trini-tarian theology of revelation. Revelation, in his view, had its beginnings in the eternal Word, the perfect Image of the Unbegotten. The Incarnation, for Mersch, was a created pro-longation of the intratrinitarian procession of the Word. Since he who became man is the divine Word, incarnation is neces-sarily revelation. In his very person Christ is the Word of God addressed to the human race, and outside of him no revelation is possible.[13]

Revelation, according to Mersch, cannot be scrutinized from outside, like an object. It is simply an aspect of the communica-tion of divine life, which is given to believers through Christ the unique Mediator. Yet the formulas in which revelation is articulated play a vital part in the Christian life. "In Christ and in the consciousness He has as head [of the Mystical Body] there are found a superabundance and a kind of pressure of fullness that flow into His members through doctrines and formulas."[14] Just as the soul cannot come into existence without the body, so the life of faith cannot come into being without sensible signs, words, and gestures. The words spoken by Christ are "the outer, corporeal aspect of a fellowship with pure eternal

12. See especially his celebrated article, "Les yeux de la foi," *Recherches de science religieuse* 1 (1910) 241–59, 444–75.
13. *Theology of the Mystical Body* (St. Louis, 1951) 381.
14. *Ibid.,* 408.

light and with the Word of God who was made flesh."[15] The words "are spirit and life, not because they are syllables and sounds, but because they are the outer, corporeal aspect of the life that communicates itself interiorly, the life of Christ, light of light who sheds light over those who belong to Him."[16]

So, too, in the Church, Mersch contended, the mystery of the incarnate Word continues to be actualized. Thanks to the divine adoption, the faithful know the triune God by sympathy and connaturality. Incorporated in the Son, they attain some understanding both of his message and of themselves. For God's message reveals them to themselves.

Mersch's profound and inspiring speculations on Christian revelation made little impact on the standard treatments of the subject in seminary manuals and popular theology, which remained imprisoned in the poverty of a rationalistic apologetics. But in the very different atmosphere prevailing since Vatican II, his ideas may at length flow into the mainstream of Catholic thinking. They coincide on many points with those of Karl Rahner, for example.

C. Germany: Kerygmatic Theology and Personalism

In the years between 1936 and 1940, several Jesuit theology professors at Innsbruck (including J. A. Jungmann, H. Rahner, and F. Lakner) became profoundly discontented with the barrenness of the prevailing school-theology. Finding the latter not meaningful for the life of faith, they proposed a new type of theology, called "kerygmatic," which would co-exist with Scholastic theology, but differ from it by being primarily oriented toward preaching. This new theology would draw more heavily on the Bible and the Patristic tradition, and would be centered on the mystery of God's self-communication in Christ rather than on the deity in itself. While Scholastic theology was

15. *Ibid.*, 410.
16. *Ibid.*, 413.

chiefly concerned with the true, kerygmatic theology would be oriented rather toward the good.[17]

The proposal of dividing theology into two such separate disciplines has not generally been well received. As Karl Rahner and others have remarked, the intention to draw up a theology more closely related to Christian experience and to the demands of living was entirely justified; the Scholasticism of the day was deficient on this score. On the other hand there was no justification for the assumption that there could be *any* legitimate theology which would be purely theoretical and divorced from pastoral concerns. The "kerygmatic" theologians seem to have themselves been trapped into an excessively objectivist notion of revelation and of science. Since revelation is God's saving message to man, and since theology is a reflection on revelation, it follows that theology must always be oriented toward the saving encounter with God who comes to us by his Word.[18] This existential and pastoral dimension is not antithetical to rigorous and disciplined thought. As Mersch and others were demonstrating, theology can be Christocentric and spiritual in emphasis without ceasing to be, in its own way, highly scientific.

Thanks to the biblical revival, the liturgical movement, and renewed contact with Protestant thought, Catholic theology in Germany began to emerge from its scholastic isolation. As one illustration of this healthy movement, the work of Romano Guardini (1885–1968), the great preacher and liturgist, deserves to be recalled. In a brief monograph on revelation, he outlined a biblical approach which was concrete, historical, dynamic and personalistic. The tone of this splendid little book is set by the opening paragraph:

The first sentence of any doctrine of revelation reads: what revelation is, revelation alone can tell. It forms no step in the sequence of

17. Two of the principal programmatic works of kerygmatic theology have recently appeared in ET: J. A. Jungmann, *The Good News Yesterday and Today* (New York, 1962) and Hugo Rahner, *A Theology of Proclamation* (New York, 1968).

18. Cf. Karl Rahner, "Kerygmatische Theologie," *Lexikon für Theologie und Kirche* (rev. 1961) 6:126.

natural disclosures of reality, but comes from a pure, divine origin. Nor is it any necessary self-communication of the supreme Being, but a free activity of the personal God. To explore the nature of this event, therefore, we must go to the school of the Bible, and be content rather to run the risk of understanding God too anthropomorphically than that of depicting him too philosophically. "God reveals" means first of all, "God acts." This action encounters man as he is and puts him, with all his merits and defects, under judgment; it demands that he should be converted, and raises him, if he obeys, to a new beginning. His obedience, indeed, is already the beginning, for the same God who calls him gives him likewise the power to obey. Thus it belongs to the essence of revelation that it cannot be deduced from the world, but that it must be accepted by reason of itself.[19]

In the remainder of this attractive essay, Guardini goes on to develop from biblical foundations an interpersonal doctrine of revelation as an historical encounter mediated through symbols. In authors such as Guardini, Catholic theology began to reap the harvest sown in the personalist philosophy of Ebner and Buber. Catholic philosophers such as August Brunner and Hans-Eduard Hengstenberg, and Catholic theologians such as Michael Schmaus, Karl Rahner, and Otto Semmelroth, were associated with this movement.[20] In some respect their work parallels that accomplished by Protestants such as Emil Brunner in the previous decade.

D. France in the Aftermath of World War II

While the German-speaking theologians were turning from Scholasticism toward more historically and personalistically oriented views, similar forces were at work in France. These currents may be illustrated in Teilhard de Chardin and in the Jesuit professors of Lyon-Fourvière.

19. *Die Offenbarung: ihr Wesen und ihre Formen* (Würzburg, 1940) 1.
20. Cf. Bernhard Langemeyer, *Der dialogische Personalismus in der evangelischen und katholischen Theologie der Gegenwart* (Paderborn, 1963).

1. TEILHARD DE CHARDIN

Pierre Teilhard de Chardin, S.J. (1881–1955), although primarily a paleontologist, pondered long and deeply on the relationship between faith and science. Although he had some contacts with Blondel through his friend Auguste Valensin, S.J., and maintained a lifelong correspondence with the Louvain dogmatician and missiologist, Pierre Charles, S.J., Teilhard was too independent a thinker to be located within any theological school. When he spoke of revelation, he normally meant the teaching of the Bible and of the Church, which he fully accepted. He found special significance in those New Testament texts (such as Col. 1:15–20) which portrayed Christ as the principle of unity and finality in the entire universe. Christ, he believed, had not merely touched the universe at a particular point in space and time, but had penetrated it to the depths and in some sense divinized the world. To the believing Christian, he maintained, "the divine milieu [that is, Christ] discloses itself to us as a modification of the deep being of things."[21] In coming into the world, God did not alter the empirical relationships between things, but added a new dimension, and made the world translucent to himself. "The world appears to the Christian mystic bathed in an inward light which intensifies its relief, its structure, and its depth."[22] The great mystery of Christianity, therefore, is not so much the "epiphany" as the "diaphany" of the divine. Christ made God accessible everywhere to those who had eyes to see.

Teilhard was convinced, moreover, that the divine light had somehow touched all men and was reflected not in Christianity alone but in the other religions. In our age, he added, the various religions were moving toward convergence. "A general convergence of the religions toward a universal Christ who, in principle, satisfies them all: this appears to me to be the only conversion possible for the world and the only possible form

21. *The Divine Milieu* (New York, 1960) 110.
22. *Ibid.*

147

of a religion of the future."[23] On the other hand he was quite emphatic in saying that Christianity was the axis toward which all must converge in order to move forward into the new age; it was the phylum of human religion which held in trust the spiritual future of mankind. "Only one religious stream in sight today is capable of answering to the demands and aspirations of modern thought; only one religion today is both possible and phyletic: Christianity."[24]

The theological writings of Teilhard, during his lifetime, were circulated only in the form of private manuscripts. He made no pretension of being a theologian, but some saw analogies between his doctrine and that of the Jesuit professors of Lyon-Fourvière, such as de Lubac, Bouillard, and Daniélou.

2. THE JESUITS OF LYON-FOURVIÈRE

Henri de Lubac, S.J. (1896–   ), a specialist in medieval theology, rediscovered in the pre-Scholastic period many themes which he found attractive and enriching. This led him to meditate fruitfully on the problem of historical relativity in the restatement of dogma. His conclusions are pointedly summarized in a famous article on the development of dogma.[25] He maintained that Charles Boyer, S.J., and others erred in seeking to show that new dogmas arose by logical deduction from earlier doctrinal formulations. This view rested on the fallacious assumption that revelation could be exhaustively stated in doctrinal formulas. The original deposit of revelation, according to de Lubac, consisted in a concrete and vital adherence to the person of Christ. He himself was the totality of dogma ("*le Tout de Dogme*"), the first and the last, and hence the unsurpassable. The mystery of Christ, to which the apostles bore witness, was

23. "Comment je crois" (unpublished essay, 1934) final sentence.
24. *Science et Christ* (Paris, 1965) 144.
25. "Le problème du développement du Dogme," *Recherches de Science Religieuse* 35 (1948) 130–60.

never a mere object of intellectual assent. Rather it was a new creation, a summons to the kingdom, perceptible only to those who allow themselves to be converted by it. Echoing Rousselot, de Lubac remarked that revelation gives new eyes to those who accept it, and unfolds before them the vista of a new universe.

A disciple and colleague of de Lubac at Fourvière, Henri Bouillard, S.J. (1908–), expressed similar views in the conclusion to his published doctoral dissertation on St. Thomas Aquinas's doctrine of justification. Historical theology, in his view, manifested the conditioned nature of doctrinal affirmations, "the relativity of the notions, the evolution of problems, and the temporary obscuring of certain important truths."[26] From his investigation of Thomas's doctrine of grace he drew the lesson:

Christian truth never subsists in its pure state. This does not mean that it must inevitably be presented mingled with error, but that it is always imbedded in contingent notions and schemes which determine its rational structure. It cannot be isolated from them. It can be liberated from one system of notions only by passing into another. Thus in order to renounce the view that the *ultima dispositio* depends on habitual grace, one must attribute it to the divine *motio.* . . . Thus the divine truth is never accessible prior to all contingent notions. Such is the law of incarnation.

History does not, however, lead to relativism. It enables one to grasp, in the midst of the theological evolution, an absolute. Not indeed an absolute of representation, but an absolute of affirmation. If the notions, methods and systems change with time, the affirmations in them remain, even though they are expressed in different categories.[27]

A third member of the theological faculty of Fourvière, Jean Daniélou, S.J. (1905–), likewise indulged in dogmatic reflections on the lessons of historical theology. Daniélou made his principal contributions in the fields of patrology and early Church history, but he kept in lively contact with modern move-

26. *Conversion et grâce chez S. Thomas d'Aquin* (Paris, 1941) 211.
27. *Ibid.*, 220.

ments, even external to the Catholic Church, especially in biblical studies and in the theology of history. In several of his works he sketched the outlines of an engaging and many-faceted theology of revelation. These may be conveniently studied in his *God and the Ways of Knowing* (1954; ET 1957).

Without aspiring to any great originality, Daniélou gracefully synthesized some of the finest insights of Scheler and Buber, Otto and Eliade, Barth and Cullmann, while at the same time correcting these authors at points where he felt that their views diverged from Catholic orthodoxy. In the pagan religions Daniélou finds a form of cosmic revelation, clouded, no doubt, but not wholly obscured, by human error. God's self-affirmation through nature, in his view, constitutes his initial self-disclosure and hence the point of departure for positive, biblical revelation. In the Bible God reveals himself by a series of singular, historical acts, making up the history of salvation. The stages of salvation history are marked by a series of covenants, such as those of Noah, Abraham, Moses, and finally the definitive covenant of the New Testament.

God's acts in history, according to Daniélou, are knowable not by ordinary observation, but only with the help of a divine activity within the human spirit. The prophets, as God's witnesses, effectively proclaim his word. The Word of God puts us in contact with the realities of salvation history and, through them, with the Triune God in his sovereign mystery. The self-revelation of the hidden God may be called, in Otto's famous term, *mysterium tremendum*. It overawes and disconcerts those to whom it comes, but at the same time thrills and fascinates them. As a patrologist, Daniélou is struck by the way in which some of the Eastern Fathers, particularly Chrysostom, analyzed the phenomenology of the holy in much the same terms as Otto. Every Christian believer, according to Daniélou, undergoes something analogous to the type of experience so splendidly described by the saints and mystics. "The testimony of those who have thus touched God contains such astonishing evidence that it becomes, even for those who

150

have not shared in it, one of the reasons for believing in God."[28]

In an article that was to become a storm center of controversy,[29] Daniélou undertook to summarize the new orientations of Catholic theology. In the first part of the article he noted with regret that an atmosphere of fear had for some time reigned in the Church as a result of the Modernist crisis. But repression alone could not avert the danger. For Modernism to be overcome, theology would have to answer to three demands:

It must treat God as God, not as an object, but as the Subject par excellence, who manifests himself when and as he pleases, so that theology must be first of all steeped in the spirit of religion; secondly, it must take account of the experiences of the modern mind and reckon with the new dimensions which science and history have given to space and time, and which literature and history have given to the soul and to society; thirdly, it must identify itself with a concrete attitude before existence; it must prove itself to be a single response which engages the whole man and the inner light of an action in which the whole of life is involved.[30]

In the theology of the past few decades, Daniélou noted with satisfaction an invigorating return to the three sources constituted by the Bible, the Fathers of the Church, and the liturgy. What was still lacking was a sufficient contact with contemporary thought. The world of Scholastic theology was still the static world of immobile essences, inherited from classical Greek philosophy. In a thinker such as Teilhard de Chardin, Daniélou found signs that it was possible for Catholic theology to accept a dynamic, evolutionary view of the universe. And in the existentialism of Gabriel Marcel he was pleased to note that God was beginning to be treated once more as personal mystery. Thanks to such leaders Daniélou felt it possible to predict a great revitalization of Catholic theology.

28. *God and the Ways of Knowing* (New York, 1957) 216.
29. "Les orientations présentes de la pensée religieuse," *Etudes* 249 (1946) 5–21. Regarding the aftermath of this article one may consult J. M. Connolly, *The Voices of France* (New York, 1961) 176–90.
30. "Les orientations . . ." 7.

3. THE REACTION; "HUMANI GENERIS"

The defenders of classical orthodoxy were not slow to take up arms against what they labelled the *"nouvelle théologie."* The editor of the *Revue Thomiste,* Michel Labourdette, O.P., launched the counteroffensive with a vigorous attack on the supposed "return to the sources." He scored de Lubac for preferring the vague symbolism of patristic spirituality to the exacting logic of scholasticism and Daniélou for leaning toward religious experience rather than adhering to conceptual precision. In Bouillard he found a dangerous surrender to historical relativism, which he labelled as one of the persistent temptations of the modern mind.[31]

In the same year the venerable Father Garrigou-Lagrange publised an article, "La nouvelle théologie où va-t-elle?"[32] He energetically rejected Bouillard's contention that it was possible to change the notions contained in a conciliar definition while at the same time remaining faithful to the sense of the affirmation. Teilhard's evolutionary doctrine of "Christogenesis" was in his eyes pantheistic and Hegelian; he dismissed it as Christian in name only. The new theology, he concluded, comes down to nothing other than Modernism. By substituting a vitalist and evolutionary notion of truth for the immutable truth of perennial theology, it opened the doors to total relativism.

The controversy continued for several years, with some theologians defending and others attacking the "new theology," until August 12, 1950, when Pius XII issued the encyclical, *Humani generis.* On the whole, this encyclical may be described as a censure of those "innovating theologians" (none were mentioned by name) who were seeking to by-pass the acquisitions of Scholastic theology and to regress to the language of Scripture and the Fathers. In particular, it deplored the view of some Catholics that dogma should be restated in terms of modern philosophies, whether immanentist, idealist, or ex-

31. "La théologie et ses sources," *Revue Thomiste* 46 (1946) 353–71.
32. *Angelicum* 23 (1946) 126–46.

istentialist. With evident disapproval, the encyclical referred to the view, occasionally propounded, that "after all, the mysteries of the faith can never be expressed in terms which exhaust the truth—only in approximate terms, perpetually needing revision, which adumbrate the truth up to a point, but suffer, inevitably, from a kind of refraction."[33] Against such "relativism" the encyclical maintained that, while the terms in which the faith had been expressed were always susceptible of further perfecting, the common teaching of the schools rested upon principles and ideas inferred from "a just apprehension of all created things" under the guidance of the divinely directed magisterium of the Church. Thus the net result of the encyclical was strongly favorable to Scholastic theology. In its concluding paragraphs *Humani generis* went on to exalt the philosophy of the Schools, praising it for its firm grasp of the unassailable principles of metaphysics, namely those of sufficient reason, causality, and finality.

While *Humani generis* was unquestionably adverse to the new theology, its language was so general as to be scarcely restrictive. Some interpreted it as a condemnation, but others, perhaps more correctly, as a warning against extremes which had not been embraced by the theologians we have mentioned. In the perspectives of history, the most important elements of the encyclical may prove to be its concessions rather than its affirmations. While asserting the capacity of human reason to establish the preambles of faith, including the existence of God, the pope recognized the indispensability of moral dispositions and the important role of knowledge "by connaturality." While defending the validity of Scholastic theology, he praised the biblical movement, and noted that theology grows barren when it does not constantly nourish itself from the original sources. While urging caution in embracing the tenets of the new philosophies, Pius XII urged theologians to "devote careful study to any new problems which our modern culture, and the progressive

33. The encyclical *Humani generis* (R. A. Knox trans.) *The Tablet* (London) 196 (1950) 188.

spirit of the age, may raise."[34] Thus *Humani generis,* while it merits to be called a conservative pronouncement, was not reactionary or repressive. If the encyclical has acquired a bad name, this is partly because some interpreted it with excessive rigidity.

E. The Magisterium and Biblical Studies

Although the problems concerning the authority and interpretation of Scripture do not lie within the scope of the present historical sketch, the persistent controversies in this field significantly affected the atmosphere in which theological speculation had to move. Naïve acceptance of the Bible as the "revealed word of God" was undermined, to a great degree, by the advances of the natural and historical sciences in the nineteenth century. Modernism was ready to accept the domination of scientific historical method in biblical studies. Conservative theology reacted by insisting vehemently on the integral inspiration and total inerrancy of the Bible, and on the binding character of traditional Catholic interpretations. The biblical encyclicals of Leo XIII (*Providentissimus Deus,* 1893) and Benedict XV (*Spiritus Paraclitus,* 1920) were on the whole conservative in tenor, as were the numerous "replies" issued by the Pontifical Biblical Commission between 1905 and 1916.

By the time of Pius XII, the Pontifical Biblical Commission and the Pontifical Institute of Biblical Studies had become staffed by exegetes committed to the validity of scientific biblical scholarship. This produced something of a crisis. Some reactionary Catholics identified the philological, historical, and archaeological examination of the Bible with naturalism, Modernism, and skepticism, and advocated a type of "spiritual exegesis" which relied on prayerful recourse to the Holy Spirit. Pius XII in his encyclical *Divino afflante Spiritu* (1943) came to the defense of critical biblical scholarship, as it had evolved in the fifty years since *Providentissimus Deus,* and en-

34. *Ibid.,* 190.

couraged Catholic exegetes to pursue their investigations without fear of harassment. Recognizing that the ancient Israelite authors wrote in forms and style no longer familiar to us, the encyclical called for careful study of the biblical literary genres. *Divino afflante Spiritu* has justly been called the "magna charta" of Catholic biblical scholarship.[35] While its concessions were later hedged with cautious admonitions by *Humani generis,* this encyclical struck a blow for scientific honesty and went far to expel the spirit of defensiveness that had reigned in the Church since the Modernist crisis.

The struggle between conservative and liberal biblical scholarship, however, continued in the reign of John XXIII. In a Monitum of 1961 the Holy Office expressed concern over opinions which would call into question "the historical and objective truth of Sacred Scripture." But in 1964 the Biblical Commission issued a remarkably progressive instruction which acknowledged that the gospels give us the words and deeds of Jesus only as filtered through a generation of oral tradition and as fitted into the redactional framework constructed by the Evangelists themselves.[36] These advances in official Catholic teaching concerning the Bible were to be consolidated in the Vatican II Constitution on Divine Revelation, especially chapters 3 and 5.

F. Vatican Council II

The Vatican II Constitution *Dei Verbum* derives, for the most part, from a schema on the "Sources of Revelation" debated at the first session (October, 1962) and withdrawn by order of John XXIII. The document ultimately adopted by the Council in November, 1965, was drafted by a mixed commission, most of whose members were drawn either from the Theological

35. For the historical importance of this encyclical, see J. Levie, *The Bible Word of God in Words of Men* (New York, 1961) 126–90.

36. See J. A. Fitzmyer, *The Historical Truth of the Gospels* (The 1964 Instruction of the Biblical Commission) (Glen Rock, N.J., 1965).

Commission or from the Secretariat for Christian Unity. Unquestionably the most important official statement ever issued by the Catholic Church on the subject of revelation, it merits careful study.

Since the text is readily accessible, there is no need to summarize it here. But it may be helpful to reproduce, in part, the explanation of the first chapter given on the Council floor on September 24, 1964, by Archbishop Florit. This "relatio" throws a clear light on the intention of the Commission which composed the text. With reference to paragraph 2, on the nature and object of revelation, Florit stated:

As regards the nature of Revelation, it is said to be of divine origin, chiefly because it begins unconditionally from God and is carried forward by him.

In his revelatory action God is impelled by his goodness and wisdom, rather than solicited by the impotence and need of men. Thus the fact of revelation has a primarily theocentric character.

The constitutive elements of revelation are both the deeds wrought by God in salvation history and the words by which God himself wills his works to be explained. Hence appears the historical and sacramental character of revelation: historical, because it consists primarily in all the interventions of God, which are designated by the name "economy" insofar as they are unified by the single aim of procuring the salvation of man; sacramental, moreover, because the total significance of the deeds is not known to us except by words, that is, by the "speech of God," which is itself a historical event.

As regards the object of revelation, first, God himself is to be considered insofar as he reveals himself through the salutary works which he has done, and which are brought to a head in the supremely salutary event of the Incarnation of the Word, whereby Christ truly pertains to the history of every age. The logically secondary object, which however accompanies and perfects the history of salvation, is the speech of God, by which we learn the truth both about God and about the salvation of men. Inasmuch as God has become our brother and mediator in Christ, this truth is by no means exhausted in the intellectual order, but it demands that, in and through Christ, it should be reduced to practice, through communion with the most blessed Trinity: which therefore is a truly interpersonal communion.

After a brief discussion of article 3, on the preparation for the gospel in the Old Testament, Florit went on to amplify the supremely revelatory quality of the Christ event, as explained in article 4. Christ, he said, became the final and unsurpassable self-revelation of God by his words and works and indeed by all that he was and is.

The remainder of *Dei Verbum* is devoted to the discussion of divine tradition and of the authority and use of Scripture. To analyze these chapters would take us far afield. One may say, however, that "although the important controversies at the Council centered on positions contained in these other chapters, the *punctum saliens* of the Constitution is the new concept of revelation."[37] Since revelation is no longer regarded as a set of doctrines but primarily as a person who comes to us in grace and love, it is possible, as Baum says, "to come to a broader understanding of scriptural inspiration and inerrancy and to a less literal concept of the historicity of the biblical books."[38] The new concept of revelation is well indicated by Latourelle. Commenting on the quotation from 1 Jn. 1:2–3 in the preamble, he writes: "This text of St. John's describes the whole movement of revelation: the *life in God,* the life which *descends* towards man, and, in Jesus Christ, is *manifest* to man in order to effect his return to Life."[39] The view of revelation proposed by *Dei Verbum* may be characterized as concrete rather than abstract, historical rather than philosophical, biblical rather than scholastic, ecumenical rather than controversial, interpersonal rather than propositional.

Dei Verbum was in substance composed before the second session of the Council. In other documents written during the second and third sessions, especially the Pastoral Constitution

37. Gregory Baum, "Vatican II's Constitution on Revelation: History and Interpretation," *Theological Studies* 28 (1967) 75.
38. *Ibid.*
39. *Theology of Revelation,* 457.

on the Church in the Modern World (*Gaudium et spes*), one finds hints of a wider view of revelation, with greater stress on the secular and cosmic dimensions. Christ is asserted to "reveal man to himself" and to make "the riddles of sorrow and death grow meaningful."[40] *Gaudium et spes* declares, further, that "all believers of whatever religion have always heard his [God's] revealing voice in the discourse of creatures."[41] Nor does this Constitution limit God's revealing activity to the times long past, as *Dei Verbum* might seem to do. It says that God, "revealing himself to his people to the extent of a full manifestation of himself and his incarnate Son, has spoken according to the culture proper to different ages."[42] Indeed he continues to speak to man through the life of the Church and the events of world history. A primary task of the Church, according to *Gaudium et spes,* is to discern the signs of the times and to interpret the many voices of our age, judging them in the light of the divine Word.[43] The Pastoral Constitution, with its positive orientation toward contemporary secular history, implicitly affirms that revelation is a continuing process, and that it must be newly expressed for every age in prophetic witness. The Council did not spell out the concept of revelation underlying documents such as *Gaudium et spes,* but it is fair to say that these documents "rest upon a more developed notion of revelation than that which has yet surfaced."[44]

G. Rahner

The most powerful restatement of the Catholic theology of revelation for the period in which the Church finds itself on

40. *Gaudium et spes,* art. 22, nos. 1 and 7, in W. M. Abbott (ed.), *The Documents of Vatican II* (New York, 1966) 220, 222.

41. *Ibid.,* art. 36, no. 5; Abbott ed., 234.

42. *Ibid.,* art. 58, no. 1; Abbott ed., 264.

43. *Ibid.,* art. 44, no. 4; Abbott ed., 246. Cf. art. 4, no. 1; Abbott ed., 201.

44. G. Moran, "The God of Revelation," in D. Callahan (ed.), *God, Jesus, and Spirit* (New York, 1969) 7.

the morrow of Vatican Council II is unquestionably to be found in the writings of Karl Rahner, S.J. (1904–   ). After nearly twenty years' teaching at Innsbruck in Austria, Rahner became professor of philosophy of religion at Munich for a short space (1964–67) and then transferred to the Catholic theology faculty at Münster.

The foundation of Rahner's theology consists in his philosophical anthropology, as developed in *Spirit in the World* (1939; ET 1968)[45] and *Hearers of the Word* (1941; ET 1969). Developing in an original direction certain themes found in the transcendental Thomism of Joseph Maréchal and the existential ontology of Martin Heidegger, he depicts man as the point where material being achieves freedom and responsibility in reflective presence to itself (*Beisichsein*). In every act of knowledge, Rahner maintains, man is obscurely in contact with God as the inexhaustible plenitude lying beyond all possible objects. But God appears more as question than as answer. In the absence of revelation, man could not know whether God takes an interest in man, and if so whether he will ultimately show himself as a just and merciless judge or as a loving Saviour.

Man's actual situation before God, according to Rahner, is inherently specified by his vocation to union with God in Jesus Christ. The universe, as it actually exists, is totally ordered to Christ as the "firstborn of all creatures" (Col. 1:15).[46] And because of Christ, all creation is drawn to God in a new way. Man therefore cannot be at rest except in interpersonal communion with God. This supernatural orientation toward the divine indelibly affects man's experience in this life, "the experience of infinite longings, of radical optimism, of unquenchable discontent, of the torment of the insufficiency of everything attainable, of the radical protest against death, the experience of being confronted with an absolute love precisely

45. The English edition has a helpful introduction, written by F. P. Fiorenza, situating Rahner's work in the history of modern philosophy.
46. "Current Problems in Christology," *Theol. Inv.* 1 (Baltimore, 1961) 165.

where it is lethally incomprehensible and seems to be silent and aloof, the experience of a radical guilt and of a still abiding hope, and so forth."[47] In the light of Christian teaching it becomes clear that experiences of this character are correctly interpreted in terms of the call of grace.

In fact, this human restlessness toward God is a kind of first grace and first revelation. It is an initial grace because it prepares us to accept the full grace of a freely accepted communion with God. It is an inceptive revelation because in it man can already hear, even though only in a confused way, the call to such communion.

Whenever man answers this initial call, God with his gracious gift of friendship will be present. As a communication of God's very self, grace is essentially life. A reality of the spiritual order, it necessarily has an impact on man's consciousness, giving him a new outlook, a new frame of reference. Grace in its inner luminosity is already revelation, but because man is incapable of completely reflecting on his spiritual acts, he cannot perceive this by simple introspection. Yet grace is never merely interior. Bestowed in and through a concrete historical situation, grace tends of its own accord to objectify itself in signs which express the new orientation of the human spirit.[48]

In the various religions of the world, and even in quasi-religions such as secular humanism, we have partial expressions —or "thematizations"—of what man perceives by the inner light of faith, in fidelity to his inner dynamism toward the God of grace.[49] But these expressions are normally marred by man's spiritual obtuseness and culpable distortions. Most religions therefore contain elements of superstition and idolatry.

The Judaeo-Christian tradition, according to Rahner, is a privileged phylum in which man's relationship to God is expressed without substantial error. God so gave himself to Israel

47. "Nature and Grace," *Theol. Inv.* 4 (Baltimore, 1966) 183–84.
48. "History of the World and Salvation History," *Theol. Inv.* 5 (Baltimore, 1966) 97–114.
49. "Christianity and the Non-Christian Religions," *Theol. Inv.* 5 (Baltimore, 1966) 115–34.

through his self-communication that that nation, at least in its prophetic leaders, was able to objectify its experience of God in ways that historically prepared for the coming of Christ. Christ, who prolongs in his human existence the uncreated self-expression of God as Logos, is the supreme symbolic realization of God's presence to the world. He is therefore the summit and goal of all revelation. Every other revelation is but a deficient participation of what takes place in the fullest measure in Christ.[50]

Rahner's ideas on revelation, scattered throughout numerous articles in his *Theological Investigations* and *Inquiries,* cannot easily be summarized in a few paragraphs. But from what has been said it should be clear that he has produced an imposing philosophico-theological synthesis—one that has enormous implications for theological anthropology, for Christology, for ecumenical theology, for the dialogue between the various religions, and even for the dialogue with secular humanism. Thanks to his recognition of the value of interior (or "transcendental") revelation, Rahner is able to make due allowance for religious experience and its varied expressions in man's religious history. But by insisting on the primacy of Christ and of the community which perpetuates Christ's sacramental presence in the world, Rahner protects himself from any latitudinarian relativism. While he is aware of the limitations of dogmatic statements,[51] he insists that the Church is able to thematize its experience of God in statements that are objectively true.[52]

In many respects Rahner's theology of revelation may be regarded as a Catholic answer to the problems raised by Modernism. Since revelation in his system fills a genuine need of concrete human nature, and originates in an ineffable experience, he effectively avoids the extrinsicism and irrelevance to which so many Catholic presentations have been subject. On

50. "Observations on the Concept of Revelation," in K. Rahner and J. Ratzinger, *Revelation and Tradition* (*Quaestiones Disputatae* 17) (New York, 1966).
51. "What is a Dogmatic Statement?" *Theol. Inv.* 5, 42–66.
52. "What is Heresy?" (*ibid.*) 468–512.

the other hand, Rahner, unlike the Modernists, fully safeguards the transcendence of God, the gratuity of man's call to communion with God, and the binding truth-value of dogmatic formulations.

H. Younger German-Speaking Theologians

Rahner has exercised a commanding influence on many talented younger German theologians, who have accepted and extended his theory of revelation. J. B. Metz (1928–   ), for example, in his *Christliche Anthropozentrik* (1962), developed the idea of "transcendental revelation" in terms of a metaphysical horizon-analysis similar to that of Lonergan and Coreth. Revelation, according to Metz, is never a mere object swimming into the field of the previously knowable, but an "epochal illumination" which encounters and modifies the subjective principle of understanding, thus giving man a radically new mode of understanding himself and the world (*Denkform*). Thus revelation can never be adequately described in terms of antecedent systematic criteria. It brings with itself the horizons of its own intelligibility.[53]

In a brief but important study of the Christian meaning of the non-Christian religions (*Toward a Theology of Religions,* 1964; ET, New York, 1966), Heinz Robert Schlette (1931–   ) has developed some of the theses set forth in Rahner's famous essay, "Christianity and the Non-Christian Religions."[54] He shows how it is possible for the Catholic, while asserting the absolute and universal value of Christianity, to admit the presence of revelation in the non-biblical religions, insofar as they too objectify, at a certain level, God's gracious self-communication to man in and through Christ. The grace of Christ has an influence extending far beyond the preaching and hearing of the gospel message.

Rahner's theology of salvation history[55] has been amplified

53. *Christliche Anthropozentrik* (Munich, 1962) 99–100.
54. See above, note 49.
55. See above, note 48.

and enriched by Adolf Darlapp in a number of articles, especially in his lengthy contribution to the first volume of *Mysterium Salutis*.[56] Darlapp shows how "general salvation history" is an inner moment of world history in all its length and breadth, since the grace of Christ has an impact on the consciousness of men who have not heard the name of Christ and who would perhaps not regard themselves as believers in God. In this connection, mention should also be made of Anita Röper's interesting volume, *The Anonymous Christian* (1963; ET, New York, 1966), which develops the Rahnerian doctrine that, beyond the confines of explicit, tangible Christianity, there is a wider zone of "anonymous" or latent Christianity.

Many other young and promising theologians, such as Georg Muschalek, Norbert Lohfink, and Klaus Riesenhuber, deserve mention for their work in developing Rahnerian insights pertaining to the theology of revelation. More strongly existential and personalist variants of the Rahnerian approach are being developed by Berhard Welte, who teaches at Freiburg im Breisgau, and by the Hungarian Jesuit, Ladislaus Boros, who contributes to the periodical, *Orientierung,* published at Zurich.

I. The Theology of the Word

Inspired partly by the monumental synthesis of Karl Barth, a number of recent Catholic theologians in continental Europe have sought to link the doctrine of revelation with what they call the "theology of the word." Eminent in this line is the Swiss theologian, Hans Urs von Balthasar (1905–   ), a vastly erudite thinker who seems equally at home with the Greek Fathers and German idealist poets and philosophers. His *The God Question and Modern Man* (1956)[57] has assumed new importance in the light of the current death-of-God controversies. He calls upon the contemporary Christian to open himself to the experi-

56. J. Feiner and M. Löhrer (eds.) (Einsiedeln, 1965).
57. Paperback ed. (New York, 1967) with introduction by John Macquarrie; previously published under the title *Science, Religion, and Christianity* (Westminster, Md., 1958).

ence of "the abyss of silence from which springs the Word of God"—a word which paradoxically unveils the Father who is silent in it. In several volumes of essays, notably those included in his *Word and Revelation* (ET, New York, 1964), he ponders the mystery of how Christ, as God's Word, inundates us with his presence and lures us to follow him in his self-abnegation.

In a multi-volume undertaking, *Herrlichkeit: eine theolologische Aesthetik,* Balthasar has set about constructing what he calls a "theological aesthetic," with the aim of showing how the Infinite has emerged from its ineffable transcendence so as to shine forth historically in the lives of Jesus and the saints. "The splendor of this self-revealing mystery," he writes, "cannot be compared to any other aesthetic attraction in the world."[58] With his remarkable capacity to build bridges between theology, spirituality, art, and literature, Balthasar writes in an involved, unsystematic style, and is difficult to classify. He has aroused controversy by his strong opposition to Teilhard de Chardin's evolutionary theology of history and, more recently, to Rahner's doctrine that the unevangelized are to be regarded as "anonymous Christians."

The Frankfurt professor, Otto Semmelroth, S.J. (1912–), has developed the theology of the word in its bearing on Christian preaching. In the first part of his *The Preaching Word* (1962; ET, New York, 1965), he explains how words and deeds complement each other in constituting the fullness of revelation, and how the word, besides communicating what it objectively signifies, imparts something of the speaker himself.

The Spanish Jesuit, Luis Alonso Schökel (1920–), professor at the Biblical Institute in Rome, has shown the implications of the theology of the word for biblical studies, especially in his volume, *The Inspired Word.*[59] His personalistic understanding of the word, as a medium through which God enters into communion with man, enables him to develop a flexible and credible doctrine of biblical truth and inerrancy. The truth of Scripture, he argues, is not a simple matter of

58. 1 (Einsiedeln, 1961) 110.
59. New York, 1965.

correspondence between statements and objective realities, but primarily a presence of God imparting grace through his word. This rich and original theologico-literary treatise does much to shed light on several statements in the documents of Vatican II regarding God's living presence in biblical proclamation.

J. Schillebeeckx

The Flemish Dominican, Edward Schillebeeckx (1914–   ), is in some ways comparable to Rahner for depth and power of his thought, his mastery of historical sources, and his ability to speak to the burning theological issues of the day. After the usual course in philosophy and theology in his religious order, which he pursued in Antwerp and Louvain, he taught dogmatic theology for several years and then worked for a doctorate at Le Saulchoir, under M. D. Chenu, O.P. Since 1958 he has been professor at the Catholic University of Nijmegen, Holland, and editor of the *Tijdschrift voor theologie*. Some of his more important articles on revelation have been collected in the first two half-volumes of his Theological Soundings.[60]

Schillebeeckx's epistemology, which underlies his theology of revelation, was shaped under the aegis of D. de Petter, O.P., who, like Maréchal, rejected the rationalistic conceptualism of modern Scholasticism in favor of a more dynamic and experiential approach. But whereas Maréchal and Rahner attend chiefly to the subjective dynamism of the human spirit, de Petter and Schillebeeckx ground the value of conceptual knowledge rather in the "objective dynamism" of reality, as this is encountered in experience and thus provides the matrix for conceptual knowledge.

On the basis of this epistemology, Schillebeeckx argues that revelation cannot be considered as an objective datum external to the experience in which it is given. Faith must always be interpreted in the light of contemporary life. But this does not

60. *Revelation and Theology* 1 (New York, 1967) and 2 (New York, 1968).

mean, for Schillebeeckx, that we can freely eliminate anything contained in the previous affirmations of the Church's faith, or that we may proceed to construct a new faith on the basis of our own experience. On the contrary, revelation is founded on the acts of God in salvation history, which reached their unsurpassable climax in the Christ-event of the first century. These divine acts, however, do not become revelation for us except as they have been interpreted and are made present to us through the word of God. The inspired interpretation given by the prophets and apostles has been faithfully condensed in the written words of Scripture. The full meaning of Scripture is not accessible to neutral, scientific exegesis, but only to one who goes to the text in the light of a contemporary experience of God. Such a reader is in a position to grasp not only the superficial literal sense, but the profound meaning of the Bible—its *sensus plenior*. For him the biblical words have an "objective dynamic force" that unveils new and unsuspected depths. The development of dogmas, for Schillebeeckx, is a process of explicitation of meanings vaguely and latently present in the Bible from the beginning.

Schillebeeckx's doctrine of revelation rests on an intriguing combination of classical Thomism and modern existential phenomenology. His theological hermeneutic is reminiscent of Heidegger's efforts to "retrieve" the deeper meaning in the works of the pre-Socratic philosophers. Whether or not the method is valid, Schillebeeckx is unquestionably making a bold and constructive attempt to meet the problems posed by Modernism. He offers a sophisticated method of restating the content of revelation in such a way that it can function existentially in the new contemporary self-understanding. If he is correct, this translation can be accomplished without any whittling away at the ancient deposit of faith.

K. North American Authors

While American theology, especially in Catholic circles, has hitherto been little more than a faint echo of ideas previously

166

enunciated in Europe, there are indications in our time that the Church is coming of age in the Western hemisphere. The dominant trend in North America is experiential, evolutionary, and pragmatic. The concerns are similar to those of Schille-beeckx, but the philosophical orientations are on the whole less metaphysical.

In Canada the young lay philosopher, Leslie Dewart, of St. Michael's College in the University of Toronto, exhibits these tendencies in his much-discussed *The Future of Belief* (1966). In an utterly radical manner, he argues that Christianity must be de-Hellenized and de-ontologized in order to align itself with the experience of contemporary man. Revelation, in his view, must no longer be regarded as a message or a doctrine. It is an event that happens today, through God's present self-communication. Revelation was complete in the first century in the sense that the "new and eternal" covenant was established in Christ; but within the era of the Incarnation, God's self-revelation, and the dogmas by which human consciousness ex-presses and formulates its meaning, continue to evolve. If they did not, Dewart argues, revelation would no longer be a reality, but simply a memory of the past. The Christian, from a stand-point within faith, experiences God as present, although not, of course, as an empirical fact. "It is always possible to look at the same facts and to find nothing but the absence of God."[61] The believing Christian must inevitably conceptualize his ex-perience, but he does not have to accept concepts formulated in the past, such as the Scholastic notion of God as a super-natural Being. What is essential is that he should experience God as an expansive force impelling him to generous service.

While some have found fault with Dewart's book on the ground that it neglects to set forth a coherent epistemology, and rests on a deficient doctrine of truth, it is evident that he is working on problems central to a modern theology of revela-tion.[62] The widening gap between verbal orthodoxy and con-temporary forms of experience, pointed out by Dewart, is a

61. *The Future of Belief* (New York, 1966) 178.
62. Cf. G. Baum (ed.), *The Future of Belief Debate* (New York, 1967).

matter of concern to a growing number of Catholic intellectuals in the United States. Gabriel Moran and Eugene Fontinell may be taken as representative.

Gabriel Moran, F.S.C., first made himself known to the theological community through his concise and penetrating little study, *Scripture and Tradition.*[63] At the end of this work he pointed out that the question whether *all* revelation is contained in the Bible cannot be answered until one has dealt with the prior questions, what is revelation and how is *any* revelation contained in the Bible? In his *Theology of Revelation,* he propounded the view that revelation is essentially "a personal union in knowledge between God and a participating subject in the revelational history of a community."[64] Putting the accent on personal encounter, he tends to a somewhat actualistic position, and evaluates the historical and doctrinal aspects of revelation almost entirely in terms of their power to contribute to a present existential communion with God. Having reached its abiding fullness in the consciousness of the risen Christ, revelation continues to be given in the history of the Church and of the world.

Moran has rather independent views on the manner in which revelation should be taught. His *Cathechesis of Revelation*[65] emphasizes the need of proportioning religious instruction to the needs and capacities of the student, neither overburdening him with exegetical and doctrinal materials which have no religious meaning for him, nor demanding a fullness of commitment which his youth cannot yet sustain. Moran's observations on making catechesis relevant to the contemporary American adolescent offer a clear and forceful challenge to the biblical-kerygmatic approach that has been prevalent in Catholic catechetical practice since the 1950's.

In a number of recent articles, Moran has begun to speak with a radicalism not apparent in his earlier work. While admitting that there is a God who is in the *process* of revealing,

63. New York, 1963.
64. *Theology of Revelation* (New York, 1966) 93.
65. New York, 1966.

he rejects the idea that Christ delivered any revealed truths or that Christians can lay claim to any knowledge inaccessible to the rest of men. "The distinctive character of Judaic-Christian revelation is that God has left us no revelation."[66] The Christian, therefore, must renounce every effort to deliver any message, whether dogmatic or biblical. "Other religions demand that men accept this or that thing. Christianity only invites men to accept themselves and their own freedom in a community with God."[67]

Moran's position is actually more nuanced than these isolated sentences would suggest. He protests quite rightly against any tendency to look on revelation as something in man's possession or at his disposal. He insists that our knowledge of God, especially within faith, is elusive. "God reveals and conceals himself in the naming of every truth."[68] In the Incarnation, God does not become obvious or comprehensible but, on the contrary, more paradoxical than ever before.

Approaching the theology of revelation from the tradition of James and Dewey, Eugene Fontinell, chairman of the philosophy department of Queens College, New York, speaks in somewhat the same terms as Dewart and Moran. He goes beyond Moran in insisting that faith is not knowledge—not even a special mode of knowledge—but rather an integrating experience which serves to order and illuminate human life, giving it meaning and direction. Religious truth, in his view, consists not in correspondence with an outside reality but in enabling one to participate more fully in the ongoing processive reality with which man is continuous. Creeds and dogmas, therefore, are not to be assessed in terms of the knowledge about God they are thought to convey, but in terms of their ability to help man move beyond the relatively inadequate situation in which he finds himself and to expand his life within the human community.[69]

66. "The God of Revelation," (*art. cit.*, note 44 above) 12.
67. *National Catholic Reporter*, April 13, 1966.
68. "The God of Revelation," *loc. cit.*
69. E. Fontinell, "Religious Truth in a Relational and Processive World," *Cross Currents* 17 (1967) 283–315.

If Fontinell is right, the notion of revelation, as it comes down to us through the tradition, must be radically recast. For faith, as he understands it, instead of being a reception of knowledge, is a communication of life. Yet his admission that faith does possess its own kind of truth leaves open the possibility of still speaking of revelation. He continues to accept the God of theism, even while seeking to avoid objectifying language about him.

While Fontinell is surely justified in dismissing a Lockean objectivist notion of religious truth, he has yet to make out his case for an undiluted pragmatism. Nearly all the major theologians who have dealt with the question of revelation since the Modernist crisis have been conscious of the shortcomings of crude representationalism, and have sought, in one way or another, to mitigate the subject-object dichotomy. It would be unfortunate if American theology, in its efforts to come into its own, were to isolate itself from dialogue with the theological effort that has borne such excellent fruits in Europe in the past two decades. Before the Modernist crisis can be said to have been overcome, Catholic theologians must achieve greater unanimity about the meaning of Truth in the area of revelation, faith, and religion.

6. CONCLUSION

While every believer will wish to understand revelation as fully as he can, our survey seems to indicate that no one understanding can be appropriate for all persons, times and cultures. Revelation comes to different ages and different individuals in different ways, and is assimilated only to the extent that a finite and conditioned human mind will allow. It is not surprising, therefore, that the concept of revelation has undergone numerous epochal and transcultural shifts.

A. Epochal Changes in the Idea of Revelation

Without seeking to be complete in our enumeration, we may take note of at least the following nine characteristic forms in which men have thought of revelation and its correlative, faith, from biblical times until our own generation.

1. In the Old Testament the dominant notion is that of the "Word of God" addressed to Israel through his chosen messengers. Yahweh's word is a dynamic force demanding prompt obedience and empowering men to action. It carries with it a guarantee of protection and prosperity to those who rely on it. Most centrally, then, revelation for the ancient Israelite takes the form of a covenant between Yahweh and his chosen people. It is given first of all to Israel as a nation, and only secondarily —as it were, derivatively—to individuals who become part of the covenant people.

171

Faith, on this view, is obedience to the Word of God. It involves not only intellectual assent but also firm commitment to a way of life. The certainty of faith, for the Old Testament writers, meant the true and lasting security which was the prerogative of those who placed their confidence in Yahweh. The Lord, they believed, is the powerful ally of those who put their trust in his promises and his protective might.

2. In the New Testament the covenant-notion of revelation is extended and transformed. Revelation now takes the form of the manifestation of the new and definitive covenant in Jesus as Messiah and Lord. In him the covenant promises formerly confined to Israel are made available to men of every nation, provided they as individuals accept him in faith and enter the community of believers.

Faith, in this context, is a trustful personal adherence to Jesus as Lord and Saviour, involving full commitment to his law of love.

3. In the Patristic era and in medieval monasticism revelation is primarily envisaged as the action of God inwardly enlightening the soul with an obscure but deeply satisfying anticipation of the eternal vision. Such enlightenment is differentiated from the mysticism of pagan philosophical schools insofar as the Christians maintain that the true source of light is the God of Israel and his Eternal Word.

The form of faith corresponding to this conception of revelation is primarily contemplative. It consists in docility to the divinely given light and in loving communion with the invisible God.

4. In medieval Scholasticism revelation takes the form of a body of divine doctrine furnishing answers to important questions about God, man, and the universe with which philosophy had grappled in vain. This body of doctrine, imparted to mankind by the prophets and apostles, is contained in the Bible as

172

a primary source book. Thus Moses and Christ are called upon to solve the riddles that Aristotle and Plotinus had failed to decipher.

Faith, in the Scholastic view, takes the form of an intellectual assent to revealed doctrines on the strength of God's word. The word of God, contained in the Bible, is authoritatively interpreted by the Church.

5. In the Protestant Reformation, spearheaded by Luther, we witness a certain collapse of confidence in medieval forms and structures. Revelation is seen as the response to man's anxious quest for a gracious God. It is therefore viewed as the good news that God offers salvation to sinners through the merits of Jesus Christ. This gospel message is found primarily in the New Testament, and perhaps especially in the Pauline doctrine on justification.

Faith, according to this schematization, takes the form of lively confidence that one's sins are cancelled out by God's mercy extended in Jesus Christ.

6. In the Catholicism of the Counter Reformation, the medieval view of revelation as a body of doctrine is reinforced with redoubled insistence on the role of the Church as authoritative teacher. Revelation is therefore viewed objectively as the content of the Church's doctrine, which is affirmed to be derived from Scripture and Tradition as sacred sources.

Faith, in this perspective, becomes a matter of submission to the teaching of the magisterium. All Catholics are held to "implicit faith" in whatever the Church might teach. There is correspondingly less emphasis on the New Testament theme of the salvific power of the message itself. No longer does one find central interest in the mystical dimension of faith as docility to the inner enlightenment of grace, which had meant so much to the Fathers, and even the medieval quest for speculative wisdom becomes subordinated to the concern for loyalty to the Church as an organization.

173

7. Skipping over the interesting developments in Protestant Orthodoxy and Rationalism, we may turn next to the Evolutionary Idealism of the nineteenth century. According to this school, revelation is identified with the emergence of the Absolute Spirit in history. Theologically concerned Idealists tend to look upon the appearance of Jesus Christ, the God-man, as the crucial moment of this emergence.

Faith, in the Idealist framework, meant the acceptance of the symbols of the Christian religion as valid pointers to the preeminent truth of man's ultimate unity with the divine.

8. Toward the end of the nineteenth century, individualistic moralism and sentimentalism, in combination with the development of the scientific approach to objective truth, gave birth to the Liberal-Modernist cult of religious experience as a substitute for authoritative doctrine. Revelation and faith were telescoped in such a way that both were equated with a vivid interior sense of the loving Fatherhood of God and an ethical commitment to the brotherhood of all men. Christian preaching was valued for the symbolic power with which it expressed and evoked religious experience. Jesus, as the supreme recipient of filial consciousness, was revered insofar as his experience of God was considered paradigmatic for that of all true believers.

9. In the period between the two World Wars, the doctrine of revelation was powerfully affected by existentialism. Feeling the threat of absurdity and despair, men turned to revelation to supply a center of meaning and value and to sustain them in the face of perplexing "boundary situations." Revelation therefore came to be viewed as the manifestation of that which concerns man ultimately. This was considered by Christian theologians to be given most fully through the preaching of the Cross and Resurrection, or through confrontation with the biblical picture of Jesus as the Christ.

Corresponding to this view of revelation, faith appeared as the courageous act of pinning the meaning of one's life on

174

Jesus Christ and of radical obedience to the demands of the God-encounter mediated by him.

A survey of these nine perspectival views of revelation should put us on guard against identifying revelation and faith themselves with any one theological outlook and should make as alert to detect signs of new perspectival changes in the present and in the future.

B. Contemporary Trends: Protestant and Catholic

None of the nine models we have surveyed accurately coincides with the most vital trends in the theology of our day. In the past two decades, there seem to be two main streams of thought, which may be loosely identified with Protestantism and Catholicism, provided these terms are not taken in any exclusivist denominational sense.

Protestant theology has on the whole been grappling with the meaning of history, and has focussed on revelation as a symbolic event within history which can be, and is, interpreted in such a way as to unlock the significance of the entire historical process. This view of revelation may be instanced in the writings of H. R. Niebuhr, Alan Richardson, Pannenberg, and Harvey.

Catholic theology has been more directly concerned with the divine. Its orientation has been more transcendental and metaphysical, less immanental and historical. Hence revelation has been predominantly viewed as the self-bestowal of the infinite God, insofar as his coming in grace makes an impact on man's noetic life. This theocentric view of revelation is reflected in the theology of Rahner and Schillebeeckx and in the teaching of Vatican II (*Dei Verbum*).

There is no contradictory opposition between these two approaches. The "Protestant" will be able to point out that the disclosure of the meaning of all history in the Christ-event is precisely the appearance of the divine. And the "Catholic" will

175

readily acknowledge that the divine, when it communicates itself in grace, becomes embodied in historically tangible symbols which afford clues to the ultimate meaning of the cosmic process and man's personal existence.

The general theory of revelation is not today a major barrier between Protestants and Catholics. It is quite true, however, that there are characteristic differences. Protestants, for the most part, have felt less committed than Catholics to authoritative Church teaching. As a result, they have tended to be more creative, more heavily influenced by current philosophies, and more closely attuned to the *Zeitgeist* of the moment. Catholics have been more concerned with maintaining solidarity with the total tradition—ancient and medieval as well as modern—and with speaking in such a way that they could bear common witness before the rest of the world. Hence Catholic theology has been much preoccupied with dogma and magisterial teaching.

Because of the increased fluidity and pluralism introduced into Catholicism by Vatican II, and the growing sensitivity of Protestants to the deleterious effects of rampant individualism, it seems safe to predict that the coming years will see a continuing convergence between the Catholic and Protestant theologies of revelation.

The widespread crisis of faith in all the Churches suggests that Christianity is presently passing through an important epochal change, the exact shape of which is not yet clear. What seems certain is that many of the classical positions are being challenged. Our contemporaries find difficulty in the idea of supposedly infallible, sacred sources; many are unwilling to be tied to a body of beliefs which allegedly reached completion in the first century of the Christian era; they shy away from giving unconditional credence to agencies that claim to speak decisively in the name of God; nor do they see the meaning or importance of many doctrines which their fathers and fore-fathers accepted as matters of faith. All of this could indicate that revelation itself will not continue to be a viable theological category. But it seems far more likely that the idea of revelation

176

is simply passing through another epochal change, analogous to those already noted. The theology of the future will probably be more critical of past tradition and present doctrinal standards; it may also be more pragmatically oriented and more concerned with establishing human community on earth. If these developments occur, the theology of revelation will have to accommodate itself to the general trend. A theology which could not make such adaptations would be dead or moribund.

C. Three Mentalities

In addition to the epochal changes we have just discussed, there are other variations in the idea of revelation which seem traceable rather to the personality and temperament of the individual theologian. Three basic mentalities may be distinguished, as giving rise to three distinct styles of revelational theology.

First, there is the positive or factual mind, which concentrates on revelation as concrete event—generally meaning the crucial events of biblical history, culminating in the death and resurrection of Jesus Christ. This approach characteristically gives rise to a biblicistic or kerygmatic theology of revelation. Revelation is viewed primarily as the story of the great deeds of God in salvation history. The primary medium of communication, on this view, is the reading of Scripture or, alternatively, the preaching of the good news of the gospel.

Secondly, there is the conceptual or abstractive mind, which fastens on the "eternal truths" in revelation. For this type of mind revelation is essentially a body of doctrine. According to the Scholastic view, this body of doctrine was supernaturally imparted and was, in effect, a divinely given supplement to the body of knowledge which man could obtain by his own philosophical investigations. The Rationalists and Idealists identified revelation more closely with that which autonomous reason could, in principle, achieve. On all these doctrinal views, the primary medium of communication was conceived as being

177

oral or written instruction in a situation approximating the classroom.

Thirdly, there is the intuitive or mystical approach, which tends to depict revelation as an ineffable encounter with the divine. This basic outlook may, in turn, be broken down into two subtypes, according to how the divine is discovered. Some theologians are immanentist by inclination: they experience God as one with themselves and with the world. Others are transcendental in outlook: they look upon God as the "wholly other," the "beyond." The former tend toward Monism, the latter toward Dualism.

In the view of this third class of theologians, revelation is a highly personal matter, and therefore largely incommunicable. A high value will normally be placed on symbolism and liturgy as means whereby the revelatory experience can be induced or evoked.

Parenthetically we may note that these three types of mentality have their equivalents in the field of Christian ethics insofar as man's response to revelation manifests itself in his conduct.

The positive approach tends to erect an ethic of example. This is especially evident in some of the fundamentalist sects which take the actions of Christ and of the earliest Christians as an exclusive standard of conduct, and for this reason refuse to make use of modern inventions.

The abstractive mentality tends to view morality as a matter of conformity to laws (abstract rules designed to cover all particular cases). For the Rationalists the Christian legal code is little more than a republication of the natural law; for the supernaturalists it is a supplemental norm.

The mystical-intuitive mind tends to look upon right conduct as a response to the present leading of the Spirit. It therefore embraces a charismatic ethic which can at times be antinomian (for example, in the case of the early Quakers).

In connection with the three mentalities just analyzed, it may be helpful to remark on the variety of models employed.

Believers who think of revelation in terms of one particular set of models are frequently scandalized by statements which seem quite harmless to those who think in terms of other models.

Theologians of a positivist mentality, who look upon revelation as concrete fact, are generally content to adhere, as the Bible does, to auditory models. Revelation is the "word" of God; it is a message to be loudly proclaimed and attentively heard. For the Christian, revelation is most centrally the good news of what God has done for mankind in the death and resurrection of Jesus Christ.

Those who look on revelation as doctrine tend to assimilate the relationship to some kind of teaching situation. Some cast this in authoritative terms: God, Christ, or the Church assumes the role of master; the faithful, that of pupils or disciples. Other theologians, also in the intellectualist vein, prefer to think in terms of dialogue situations. Man may be pictured as the questioner, and God as the respondent; or conversely, God may ask questions of man, reducing him to humble acknowledgment of his ignorance and to a sense of awe in the presence of the divine majesty. Where God is the questioner, revelation is no longer a matter of getting answers to questions; one passes from the intellectualist to the mystical or numinous view.

The master-disciple images, though pleasing to many intellectualists, are dissatisfying to those who profess confidence in the unaided powers of human reason. The more extreme Rationalists insist on the rights of autonomous, rather than heteronomous, reason. They tend to discard auditory and instructional imagery, and to depict revelation in visual terms. Relying on the etymology of terms such as "revelation" and "apocalypse," they would say that revelation occurs when man is able to peer into the beyond. This view of revelation tends also to satisfy those with a more intuitive approach, such as that which asserted itself in Patristic and monastic theology or in the modern cult of numinous experience.

Finally, those who shy away from Monism, and who wish to adhere faithfully to Biblical Dualism, frequently appeal to

179

personalistic and intersubjective categories. Revelation, for some of them, should be described on the analogy of the mutual disclosure and acceptance of friends or lovers.

Granted the complexity of revelation itself, the tensions between the different theological schools are desirable and even necessary. All the models have their utility, up to a point, and their dangers, if relied upon too heavily. The auditory imagery can lead to an unhealthy extrinsicism; the visual imagery, to a constricting individualism. The interpersonalistic view points up the relevance and salutary power of revelation, but, if carried to an extreme, it can obfuscate the infinite distance between God and man and overaccentuate the affective component.

Returning to the three mentalities already described, we may conclude that each has its proper contribution to make. The factual, doctrinal, and mystical components all seem to have their place in a balanced theory of revelation. Revelation is never mere fact, in the sense of a verifiable historical occurrence; it is a fact pregnant with an abiding divine significance. Revelation is never mere doctrine, in the sense of abstract propositional truth; it is always doctrine which illuminates a unique event. The event occurs not merely in the world outside man, but also within him; it has an objective and a subjective pole, neither of which can be suppressed. The most properly revelatory element would seem to be precisely the inbreaking of the divine in a manner that overcomes the subject-object dichotomy characteristic of our ordinary thought and speech.

D. Polarities and Tensions

Many other tensions and polar oppositions are apparent from the history of man's reflection on revelation. There is, for instance, the tension between fulfilment and conversion. From one point of view, revelation may be seen as the crowning of man's natural possibilities of knowledge; from another point of view, it appears as a sentence of judgment that crushes all human pretensions and requires man to make a radically new beginning "as a little child." A balanced theory must show that while revelation fulfils in a surpassing way the immanent thrust of reason, it does so in a paradoxical manner that demands a sacrifice of personal autonomy.

Then again, there is the polarity between trustful surrender and critical scrutiny. Some would look upon revelation as a demand that man relinquish all the criteria applicable to other types of knowledge; others have protested that to do so would be irresponsible and even sinful. Apologetically minded writers make much of the external criteria by which authentic revelation can be distinguished from fable and illusion; fideists reply that if objective norms were decisive, faith would lose its distinctive character as total reliance on the word of God.

Yet another tension which runs through the history of theology is that between the personal and the collective. Ecclesially minded theologians have stressed the corporate character of God's word as a message that comes to men in groups and as a force that establishes and sustains human community. Those more sensitive to the role of personal conscience stress rather the inner call of grace and the individual response to the witness of the Holy Spirit.

Finally, mention should be made of the struggle for supremacy, so acutely felt in contemporary theology, among the past, present, and future ingredients in revelation. Historically minded theologians, drawing inspiration from the Bible and ancient testimonies, look upon faith as an acceptance of God's word as deposited in sacred sources handed down from the past. A second group of theologians, more impressed by the novelty of our own times, look upon revelation as a present experience of God's Lordship in Jesus Christ. For them, past revelation would no longer be revelation for us were it not reactuated through the "continuing revelation" occurring today. A third theological school, concerned with the insufficiencies of man's existence within historical time, dwell chiefly on the futuristic and eschatological dimensions of revelation. The past and present, they tell us, would not merit the name of revelation

181

except that they point forward in promise to fuller revelation yet to come.

Many other contrasts and antitheses might be added to those just mentioned. What is essential, however, is to perceive that an adequate theology must not prematurely write off what any appreciable number of Christian believers and thinkers have regarded as important, even though this may seem difficult to reconcile with some other valid insight. Nothing is easier, or more detrimental to theology, than to reject what does not suit one's own temperament or situation, and to reduce revelation itself to some one of its aspects. Such a reduction may make for a certain specious clarity and forcefulness, but in the long run it leads to fragmentation and impoverishment.

In studying the history of man's thought about revelation one has the feeling of contemplating a spectrum in which the white light of revelation has been broken down into many bands. In this state of dispersion the various properties of revelation can be fruitfully analyzed. But after the analysis is done, there still remains the task of seeing how all these properties can be combined in a revelation which is one and undivided. To discern how the Christian revelation can be God's word and yet inhere in finite human minds; to show how it can be perfective of man and yet transcend all merely human possibilities; symbolic and yet doctrinal, mysterious and yet intelligible, real and yet verbal, social and yet personal, beyond verification and yet discernible, already given, presently actual, and still to be completed—to be able to synthesize all these apparently incompatible attributes without arbitrarily sacrificing some to others—such is the task which theology, as yet, has left unsolved. Perhaps, after all, the task of theology is not so much to solve as to continue to wrestle with these problems. Theology, in conformity with St. Augustine's famous dictum, seeks in order that it may understand; but it understands in order that it may seek still more. If we so understood that we no longer had to seek, it would not be the God of revelation that we had found.

SELECT BIBLIOGRAPHY

N.B. For the sake of wider serviceability the following bibliography is restricted to works in English of a non-technical character. Omitting original explorations into the nature of revelation, many of which are indicated in the body of the text, this list concentrates on studies of a secondary or historical character.

1. BIBLICAL VIEWS OF REVELATION

A. The Old Testament

Latourelle, René, *Theology of Revelation*. Staten Island, 1966. Part I, ch. 1.

McKenzie, J. L., *Myths and Realities: Studies in Biblical Thought*. Milwaukee, 1963.

Rad, Gerhard von, *Old Testament Theology*. New York, 2 vols., 1962, 1965.

Robinson, H. Wheeler, *Inspiration and Revelation in the Old Testament*. Oxford, rev. ed., 1946.

Wright, G. Ernest, *God Who Acts*. London, 1952.

B. The New Testament

Kittel, Gerhard (ed.), *Theological Dictionary of the New Testament*. Grand Rapids. 1964ff. Articles "kalyptō," "kēryx," "legō," etc.

Latourelle, René, *Theology of Revelation* (cited above). Part I, ch. 2.

Richardson, Alan, *Introduction to the Theology of the New Testament*. New York, 1958. Ch. 1 and 2.

Schnackenburg, Rudolf, *The Truth Will Make You Free*. New York, 1966.

2. CHRISTIANITY: THE FIRST EIGHTEEN CENTURIES

A. The Patristic Period

Latourelle, René, *Theology of Revelation* (cited above). Part II.
Ochagavia, Juan, *Visibile Patris Filius* [Irenaeus on Revelation and Tradition]. Rome, 1964.
Polman, A. D. R., *The Word of God According to St. Augustine*. Grand Rapids, 1961.
Quasten, Johannes, *Patrology*. Westminster, Md., vols. 1–3, 1950–60.
Turner, H. E. W., *The Pattern of Christian Truth*. London, 1954.

B. The Middle Ages

Gilson, Etienne, *Reason and Revelation in the Middle Ages*. New York, 1938.
Latourelle, René, *Theology of Revelation* (cited above). Part III, ch. 1.
Synave, Paul, and Pierre Benoit, *Prophecy and Inspiration* [commentary on *Summa Theol.* 2–2ae, qq. 171–178]. New York, 1961.
White, Victor, *God and the Unconscious*. Cleveland, 1961. Ch. 7 [on St. Thomas' notion of revelation].

C. The Reformation and the "Age of Orthodoxy"

Althaus, Paul, *The Theology of Martin Luther*. Philadelphia, 1966.
Dowey, E. A., Jr., *The Knowledge of God in Calvin's Theology*. New York, 1952.
Latourelle, René, *Theology of Revelation* (cited above). Part III, ch. 2.
Pelikan, Jaroslav, *From Luther to Kierkegaard*. St. Louis, 1950, 1963.

D. Deism

McDonald, H. D., *Ideas of Revelation: An Historical Study* A.D. *1700 to* A.D. *1860*. London, 1959.

Richardson, Alan, *The Bible in the Age of Science*. Philadelphia, 1961. Chs. 1 and 2.
Willey, Basil, *The Seventeenth Century Background*. Garden City, 1953.

E. Non-Conformism in England

Knox, R. A., *Enthusiasm*. New York, 1950.
McDonald, H. D., *Ideas of Revelation* (cited above).

F. Eighteenth-Century Rationalism

Collins, James, *A History of Modern European Philosophy*. Milwaukee, 1954. Chs. 8–13.
Copleston, Frederick, *A History of Philosophy*. Westminster, Md. Vol. 5 (*Hobbes to Hume*) 1959; vol. 6 (*Wolff to Kant*) 1960.
Willey, Basil, *The Eighteenth Century Background*. New York, 1941.

3. THE NINETEENTH CENTURY

A. Theologians of Feeling and Subjectivity

Barth, Karl, *Protestant Thought: From Rousseau to Ritschl*. New York, 1959. Chs. 5, 6, and 8.
Johnson, Robert C., *Authority in Protestant Theology*. Philadelphia, 1959. Part II ("The Nineteenth Century").
Niebuhr, R. R., *Schleiermacher on Christ and Religion*. New York, 1964.

B. Hegelian Idealism

Barth, Karl, *Protestant Thought* (cited above). Ch. 8.
Collins, James, *History of Modern European Philosophy* (cited above). Ch. 14.
Copleston, Frederick, *History of Philosophy* (cited above). Vol. 7 (*Fichte to Nietzsche*) 1963.
Hodgson, P. C., *The Formation of Historical Theology: A Study of F. C. Baur*. New York, 1966.

C. Trends in Nineteenth-Century Catholicism

Horton, Walter, *The Philosophy of the Abbé Bautain*. New York, 1926.

Latourelle, René, *Theology of Revelation* (cited above). Part III, ch. 3; part IV, ch. 2.

D. Liberal Protestantism

Barth, Karl, *Protestant Thought: From Rousseau to Ritschl* (cited above). Ch. 11.

Hefner, Philip, *Faith and the Vitalities of History: A Theological Study Based on the Work of A. Ritschl.* New York, 1966.

Macintosh, D. C., *The Problem of Religious Knowledge.* New York, 1940.

E. Modernism

Latourelle, René, *Theology of Revelation* (cited above). Part IV, ch. 3.

Ratté, John, *Three Modernists: A. Loisy, G. Tyrrell, and W. L. Sullivan.* New York, 1967.

Vidler, A. R., *The Modernist Movement in the Roman Church.* Cambridge, 1934.

4. TWENTIETH-CENTURY PROTESTANTISM AND ANGLICANISM

Baillie, John, *The Idea of Revelation in Recent Thought.* New York, 1956; paperback, 1964.

Baillie, John and Hugh Martin (eds.), *Revelation.* London, 1937.

Braaten, Carl, *History and Hermeneutics.* Philadelphia, 1966.

Copleston, Frederick, *A History of Philosophy* (cited above). Vol. 8 (*Bentham to Russell*) 1966.

McDonald, H. D., *Theories of Revelation: An Historical Study, 1860–1960.* London, 1963.

Macquarrie, John, *An Existentialist Theology: A Comparison of Heidegger and Bultmann.* New York, 1965.

———, *Twentieth Century Religious Thought: The Frontiers of Philosophy and Theology 1900–1960.* New York, 1963.

Ramsey, A. M., *From Gore to Temple.* London, 1961.

Richardson, Alan, *The Bible in the Age of Science* (cited above). Chs. 4–8.

Robinson, James M. and J. B. Cobb (eds.), *New Frontiers in Theology*. New York. Vol. 1 (*The Later Heidegger and Theology*) 1963; vol. 2 (*The New Hermeneutic*) 1964; vol. 3 (*Theology as History*) 1967.

Smith, Joseph J., *Emil Brunner's Theology of Revelation*. Manila, 1967.

5. CATHOLIC THEOLOGY SINCE 1910

Bea, Augustin Cardinal, *The Word of God and Mankind* [Vatican II's Constitution on Divine Revelation]. Chicago, 1968.

Bird, T. E. (ed.), *Modern Theologians: Christian and Jews*. Notre Dame, 1967.

Bulst, Werner, *Revelation*. New York, 1965.

Connolly, James, *The Voices of France*. New York, 1961.

Harrington, Wilfred and L. Walsh, *Vatican II on Revelation*. Dublin and Chicago, 1967.

Latourelle, René, *Theology of Revelation* (cited above). Part IV, ch. 4; part V, ch. 11.

Schillebeeckx, Edward (ed.), *Man as Man and Believer* (*Concilium*, vol. 21). Glen Rock, N.J., 1967.

INDEX OF AUTHORS

188